"The past does not repeat itself,
but it rhymes."

—Mark Twain

"Hip-hop is supposed to uplift and
create, to educate people on a larger
level, and to make a change."

—Doug E. Fresh

"Without education, you're not
going anywhere in this world."

—Malcolm X

FLOCABULARY STUDY GUIDES

★ Hip-Hop ★
U.S. History

Blake Harrison and Alexander Rappaport

Hip-Hop U.S. History

13-Digit ISBN: 978-1-933662-35-0
10-Digit ISBN: 1-933662-35-2

This book may be ordered by mail from the publisher. Please include $4.50 for postage and handling. Please support your local bookseller first!

Books published by Cider Mill Press Book Publishers are available at special discounts for bulk purchases in the United States by corporations, institutions, and other organizations. For more information, please contact the publisher.

Cider Mill Press Book Publishers
"Where good books are ready for press"

12 Port Farm Road
Kennebunkport, Maine 04046

Visit us on the web!
www.cidermillpress.com

www.flocabulary.com

Design: Tilly Grassa
Cover Design: Bashan Aquart
Typography: Gill Sans, Bodoni Highlight, Bernhard MT Condensed
All Illustrations and Photographs courtesy of the
Library of Congress, Prints and Photographs Division
Printed in China

1 2 3 4 5 6 7 8 9 0
First Edition

★ ★ ★ TABLE OF CONTENTS ★ ★ ★

Introduction
What Is Flocabulary? 4

The Songs
CHAPTER 1: Who Discovered It? 8
CHAPTER 2: I Want America 16
CHAPTER 3: This Ain't Working 24
CHAPTER 4: The Declaration of Independence (Interlude) 32
CHAPTER 5: It's the U.S. (Bust the A) 36
CHAPTER 6: Bill of Rights 42
CHAPTER 7: O.D.W.M. 48
CHAPTER 8: Frederick and Abraham (Interlude) 56
CHAPTER 9: Ghosts of the Civil War 60
CHAPTER 10: Big Ballin' (in the Gilded Age) 70
CHAPTER 11: Jazz Age 78
CHAPTER 12: FDR (Interlude) 82
CHAPTER 13: Would You Drop It? 84
CHAPTER 14: Let Freedom Ring 92
CHAPTER 15: Guide to the Songs 98

Appendices
I. GUIDE TO THE AGE OF EXPLORATION 106
II. GUIDE TO THE ENLIGHTENMENT 107
III. BIBLICAL REFERENCES TO SLAVERY 108
IV. CONSTITUTIONAL AMENDMENTS 110
V. DECLARATION OF INDEPENDENCE 116
VI. LIST OF U.S. PRESIDENTS 120

Acknowledgments 121

Music Credits 122

Bibliography 124

Photo and Illustration Credits 126

Introduction

History doesn't have to be boring and locked in the distant past.

This book and CD are designed to make history accessible and to make the stories of America's past come alive. U.S. history is full of amazingly dramatic and exciting moments, colorful characters, and world-changing events. It is up to us to put these stories and facts in a form that makes them feel immediate, and there is nothing more engaging or immediate than hip-hop music.

History has never been presented in this voice before. This work features some of New York City's most talented underground emcees who did more than just spit rhymes. They put their heart and soul in these verses. The experiences of history can shed powerful light on our own lives. So take it. Run with it. Bounce to it. Rap to it. Learn it. Judge it. Protest it. Know it. Discuss it. We want to challenge you from every direction.

If the Boston Tea Party were going down this weekend, would you go?

What Is Flocabulary?

Flocabulary produces educational hip-hop music to teach and engage students of all backgrounds. We truly believe that hip-hop music, when combined with a positive message and academic content, is an amazingly powerful learning tool. Not only does creative hip-hop music engage you and get your head bobbing, but the rhyming lyrics actually work as mnemonic devices to help you learn and remember. We strive to make our music as good as anything out there.

Hip-Hop U.S. History is our third project. We've also come out with Flocabulary: The Hip-Hop Approach to SAT-Level Vocabulary Building, which defines 500 SAT words in hip-hop songs, as well as The Rapper's Handbook: A Guide to Freestyling, Writing Rhymes, and Battling, a how-to guide for aspiring emcees. We offer lots of free content on our website, including how-to rap tutorials, beats for freestyling, lesson plans on hip-hop and poetry for teachers, and boards for emcees to post their rhymes. Check us out at **Flocabulary.com**.

We also perform live shows and workshops at schools and conferences throughout the nation. We're committed to changing education, and we're trying to bring our groundbreaking concept to students, teachers, and families across the world.

The Songs

CHAPTER 1

Who Discovered It?

INTRO

What is America and how do we study its origins? We have options.

We could look at America as a landmass: a vast continent of mountains, rivers, and plains stretching from the Atlantic to the Pacific. The people who discovered this America were Native Americans.

Columbus

They inhabited this land for 25,000 years before Europeans came over on giant ships.

We could also look at America as a society, a culture, and a political system. This America wasn't "discovered" by anyone. It was founded largely by ambitious Europeans who brought their capitalism, their God, their ideals, their conquering spirit, their strengths, and their weaknesses when they sailed over the seas. Then, of course, as history continued, other groups began making major contributions to form American culture. That is to say, who discovered America and who most influenced America are two different things. And this process continues.

LYRICS

Wow, I just discovered America.
You didn't discover it. We were already here.

Back before buffalo wings at Domino's,
America was where the Buffalo
roamed. What you don't know?
Thirty thousand years ago some dudes
came across the **Bering Strait**
wearing snowshoes.
Eskimos chasing woolly mammoth,
Ice Age white like dandruff.
This is the range, home of the free,
land of the brave.
They were **nomadic**, hut to hut like
quarterbacks,
hunting deer with the spear and ax.
Some tribes formed towns
and they settled down.
Domesticated plants,
oh they're farming now.
Pray for rain,
dancing on the **Great Plains**,
while mad cats with cornrows
were planting **maize**.
In the Southwest, **Anasazi** built caves.
By the **Great Lakes**, tribes,
they made blades out of **copper**.
Aztecs played games.
Lots of Indian tribes engaged in trade.
Iroquois planting squash
all up in the Northeast,

CONTEXT AND BACKGROUND

Back before buffalo wings ...
About 120,000 years ago, the Earth fell into an
ice age. Temperatures dropped, the polar ice
caps grew, and ocean levels fell. Roughly 30,000
years ago, nomadic hunting groups followed
giant herds of woolly mammoths across a land
bridge between Siberia and Alaska. These were
America's first human inhabitants.

They were nomadic ...
These first Americans were nomadic: they didn't
form permanent settlements or towns but
instead moved whenever food ran out. Around
7,000 years ago, some tribes began to farm and
settled down in permanent villages.

In the Southwest, Anasazi built caves ...
In the Southwest, the Anasazi tribe built
elaborate caves into the face of cliffs, and these
caves are still visible today. Around 3,300 years
ago, tens of thousands of Anasazi mysteriously
deserted their cliff dwellings en masse. Their
descendants (**Hopi**, **Zuni**, and others) are now
known as the **Pueblo tribes**.
  In the Mississippi area, the **Mississippi
people** became known as *mound builders*
because of the large platform mounds they
constructed for their temples.

**By the Great Lakes, tribes, they made
blades ...**
In the Great Plains, the **Cheyenne**, **Sioux**, and
other tribes hunted and foraged. They were
largely unable to hunt the mighty buffalo until
the Spanish brought horses. The tribes then
produced excellent horsemen who rode the
plains in large, powerful hunting groups.

★ FLOCAB SPITS FACTS ★ LIKE AN ALMANAC

Native Americans gave us:
- dogsleds
- words like squash, skunk, raccoon, and woodchuck
- kayaks
- The names of twenty-six U.S. states: Alabama, Alaska, Arizona, Arkansas, Connecticut, Idaho, Illinois, Iowa (the word means "this is the place"), Kansas, Kentucky, Massachusetts, Michigan, Minnesota, Mississippi, Missouri, Nebraska, New Mexico (Mexitli was an Aztec god or leader), North Dakota, Ohio, Oklahoma, South Dakota, Tennessee, Texas (means "friends"), Utah, Wisconsin, and Wyoming. (Indiana is an English word meaning "land of Indians.")
- toboggans
- totem poles
- tipi
- snowshoes
- tobacco
- lacrosse
- moccasins
- root beer

and more!

Aztecs played games . . .

Native Americans played many different sports. North American Indians invented lacrosse, and the Iroquois introduced the game to Europeans. In Mesoamerica (central and South America), Aztecs played a game called *tlachtli* on stone courts. The game resembles modern-day basketball and soccer, with players trying to hit a large rubber ball through a stone ring. The Aztecs also played board games that had ceremonial and religious meanings. According to some reports, the Spanish conquistador Hernando Cortés played a ceremonial Aztec board game with Montezuma II (the Aztec ruler) before taking him hostage.

Lots of Indian tribes . . .

By the time a man named Jesus was preaching to his followers in a faraway land, Native American tribes had spread out across North and South America. They had developed into numerous tribes that had their own distinct cultures, languages, religious beliefs, and ways of life.

In the North, the **Eskimo and Inuit** tribes developed kayaks and dogsleds to navigate the water and land. They hunted seals and whales using harpoons and used the dead animals for food, clothing, and tools.

Iroquois planting squash all up in the Northeast . . .

The Iroquois developed advanced agricultural practices, including crop rotation and the slash-and-burn technique. They cultivated beans, corn, and squash, which they called "The Three Sisters."

There were five tribes white guys called civilized . . .

What Europeans would eventually call *the five civilized tribes* lived in America's eastern

they master agriculture
with the **slash-and-burn technique**.
There were five tribes
white guys called civilized,
because of the way their government
was organized:
**Cherokee, Choctaw, Chickasaw,
Seminole,** and **Creek.**
Isn't cheap? They call my Jeep a
Jeep Cherokee?
What if they called my Jeep a Jeep Jew?
Imagine the outrage.
What would you do?

Wow, I just discovered America.
You didn't discover it. We were already here.
Wow, I just discovered America.
You ain't discovered nothing.
We was already here.

People are people, ain't nobody perfect.
Indians weren't living
on some heaven on Earth tip.
Aztecs had slaves, war in war zones,
putting holes in enemies' domes
like the ozone.
Sacrificing humans at the order of
Montezuma, the ruler.
Mayans knew dope astronomy too,
had cities with markets,
temples, and factories.
Incas had a vast empire
by today's Chile.

woodlands. The Cherokee, Choctaw,
Chickasaw, Seminole, and Creek were
considered civilized because they had
government systems that were easily
comprehended by Europeans and because
they assimilated European culture fairly easily.

In the 1700s, for example, some members of
these tribes owned plantations with slaves.
Because the term *civilized* implies that other
tribes were not, this term has been abandoned.
These tribes are now mostly known as the *Five
Tribes*, not to be confused with the Five Nations
of the Iroquois.

People are people . . .
Some people dismiss Native Americans as
savages, while others idealize their way of life.
Saying that a certain culture is good or bad,
however, is both superficial and unhelpful. It is
much more useful to study the differences
among cultures and people and judge them
within the context of their environment.

Aztecs had slaves . . .
While most tribes in North America formed
relatively modest-sized towns and nomadic
groups, Native Americans in **Mesoamerica**
developed into three huge empires: the Aztec,
the Maya, and the Inca.

The Aztec empire was centered in
Tenochtitlán, an enormous city with 100,000
inhabitants in the center of a lake. Their society
consisted of distinct social classes: nobles,
peasants, and slaves.

**War in war zones, putting holes in
enemies' domes like the ozone . . .**
The Aztecs also had a powerful standing army,
with a core of professional warriors whose rank
depended on how many prisoners of war they
had captured.

★ PERSPECTIVES ★

What about Leif Eriksson?

About 500 years before Columbus, the first "outsiders" to explore America were the Norsemen. Sailing from Iceland under the leadership of Leif Eriksson, the Norsemen explored Newfoundland in Canada and then went home.

Sacrificing humans . . .

The Aztec engaged in human sacrifice. At times, Aztecs sacrificed 1,000 people per day. One Aztec account, which is likely exaggerated, notes that during the construction of the great stone temple in Tenochtitlán, 84,000 people were sacrificed in four days.

At the order of Montezuma, the ruler . . .

Montezuma (sometimes spelled Moctezuma) was the Aztec ruler at the time the conquistadors arrived in Mexico in 1519. Hernando Cortés led the conquistadors on a rampage through Mexico, destroying villages and weakening the empire. Montezuma greeted Cortés, who then took Montezuma hostage.

Mayans knew dope astronomy too . . .

Mayan civilization flourished from 300–1000 C.E. Based primarily in the **Yucatan Peninsula**, the Mayans constructed giant temples, pyramids, palaces, and ball courts. The Mayans developed written language, studied math and astronomy, and used their astronomical measurements to create the most accurate calendar in the world at that time.

Incas had a vast empire by today's Chile . . .

Incan civilization began in today's Peru and eventually spread north to Ecuador and south to Chile. The empire flourished in the fifteenth and sixteenth centuries, expanding rapidly through military conquest and peaceful assimilation. By the time the Spanish conquistadors arrived, however, the Incan empire was over-extended, and the Spanish pitted city against city until the empire was destroyed.

The *Niña,* the *Pinta,* the *Santa Maria* . . .

Christopher Columbus had an idea. Aware that the Earth was round and that travel by sea was much easier than travel by land, he wanted to find a western route from Europe to Asia. He was looking for gold and spices, and trade routes. Spain agreed to finance his trip, and on August 3, 1492, Columbus set out on an expedition that changed the world.

Columbus departed from Spain with three boats: the *Niña* ("the little girl"), the *Pinta* ("the painted"), and his flagship, the *Santa Maria* ("the Saint Mary"). More than two months later, just as Columbus's crew was planning to mutiny and turn the ships back to Spain, a lookout spotted land. It was October 12, 2:00 A.M., and the lookout saw the moonlight reflected on white, sandy beaches. This was the New World.

Arawak greeted the crew, heated some stew . . .

This New World was not Asia (as Columbus believed), nor was it empty. Columbus had sailed to the Bahamas, and the locals swam out to greet him.

Then in the year *1492*,
 *an Italian was sent by the Spanish to find
a new route to* **India**.
His name was **Christopher Columbus**.
He was hungry for gold . . .
The **Niña**, the **Pinta**,
the **Santa Maria**.
Boats hit the **New World**
screaming out "*arriba!*"
Arawak greeted the crew,
heated some stew.
They came out bearing more gifts
than Saint Nick do.
Columbus like:
"Gather these **slaves** up quick,
lickety-split,
let's split back to Spain."
Exaggerate how much **gold** he had seen.
Came back with not three ships
but seventeen.
Columbus was a sailor and an explorer,
most of all,
Columbus was an entrepreneur.
Spanish would give him 10 percent of
all the slaves, gold,
land, and spices
that he claimed in their name.
Indians didn't know about guns and greed.
After a hundred years,
90 percent were deceased.
America is freedom, I've been told,
but I know
that it was also born of blood and gold.

These naked Arawak men and women welcomed Columbus's crew with gifts and hospitality. This is Columbus's own account of his meeting with the Arawak:

"They . . . brought us parrots and balls of cotton and spears and many other things, which they exchanged for the glass beads and hawks' bells. They willingly traded everything they owned . . . They do not bear arms, and do not know them, for I showed them a sword, they took it by the edge, and cut themselves out of ignorance."

He later described the Arawak saying that, "When you ask for something they have, they never say no. To the contrary, they offer to share with anyone."

Columbus like: "Gather these slaves up quick . . ."
One of the first things Columbus did when he arrived in America was to take some of the Arawak as slaves. He figured they could lead him to gold. At the very least they would "make fine servants." This is from Columbus's own account:

"As soon as I arrived in the Indies, on the first Island which I found, I took some of the natives by force in order that they might learn and might give me information of whatever there is in these parts . . . they would make fine servants . . . with fifty men we could subjugate them all and make them do whatever we want."

Exaggerate how much gold he had seen . . .
Columbus returned to Spain after exploring Cuba and Hispaniola. In Spain, Columbus reported to the royal court, exaggerating his findings: "Hispaniola is a miracle . . . fertile and beautiful . . . there are many wide rivers of which the majority contain gold . . . there are many spices and great mines of gold."

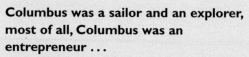

Columbus was a sailor and an explorer, most of all, Columbus was an entrepreneur ...

Columbus was an expert sailor who led an astonishingly brave expedition across the Ocean, but he wasn't sailing for science. He wanted gold. The Spanish monarchs gave Columbus the title "Admiral of the Ocean Sea" and promised him 10 percent of the gold and spices he found for them. In this way, Columbus was a businessman.

Upon his return trip to America, Columbus and his 1,500-man crew demanded that the **Taino Indians** on Hispaniola bring them gold. They established a system of quotas, in which the Indians had to bring the Spanish certain amounts of gold. If they failed to meet the quota, the Spanish would cut off their hands or, in many cases, crucify them on hilltops.

After a hundred years, 90 percent were deceased ...

The Europeans' effect on Native Americans is often glossed over in history books. The word *genocide* (the planned extermination of an ethnic group) is rarely used, probably because unlike the Holocaust, the killings were not methodical. The effect, however, was just as devastating.

A combination of greed, misunderstanding, and misplaced religious conviction led to millions of Indian deaths, but even more deadly were the diseases that Europeans brought to America. Smallpox and other diseases would eventually claim tens of millions of Indians lives. The Native American population when Columbus arrived was estimated to be around fifty million. Just one hundred years later, the Native American population was around two million.

Wow, I just discovered America.
You didn't discover it. We were already here.
Wow, I just discovered America.
You ain't discovered nothing.
We was already here.

★ ★ ★

AMERICA SPEAKS

"Endless testimonies . . . prove the mild and pacific temperament of the natives . . . But our work was to exasperate, ravage, kill, mangle, and destroy."

—Spanish priest Bartolomé Las Casas in book two of his *History of the Indies*

"Why will you take by force what you may have quietly by love? Why will you destroy us who supply you with food? What can you get by war?"

—Chief Powhatan speaking to John Smith, 1607

CHAPTER 2

I Want America

INTRO

Columbus might not have discovered America, but his journey certainly changed the world. Following Columbus, the Spanish sent out fleets of ships across oceans to discover and conquer new lands. But it wasn't until the 1600s that white settlers attempted to actually live in North America. Despite ambitious efforts, the first settlements ended badly. But after the success of the settlements in Jamestown and Plymouth, Europeans began coming to America in increasing numbers.

The natives, meanwhile, stood and watched as these strange foreigners came in on giant ships. They didn't always accept the newcomers with open arms. Bloody raids on both sides hurt the relations between Indians and Europeans. During this time, on another continent, the first Africans were being stolen from their land and shipped to America as slaves.

Pocahontas and John Rolfe

LYRICS

Planted their feet to build
a land of deceit, plot it, conquer,
and spread disease across the seas
it's the **Spanish Fleet**.
Welcome to America,
the era of early terror
where Columbus named the country
out of error.
1606, England sent **John Smith** to
lead a hundred colonists to
Jamestown, to go and conquer it.
Health became a problem
and disease would just devour
the strength of the manpower 'till it
became the final hour.
John Rolfe thought it'd be slick
to make money off of cancer sticks,
dropping **tobacco** off of his ships.
Made **Pocahontas** his chick,
converted her to **Christianity**,
brought her to England where she fell
to this calamity.
Smallpox or insanity. Is it true?
If you say can it be,
of course the next plan
will have to stand complete.
In **1619** new force, government,
set up the **House of Burgesses**

I want America, I want America!
Crisscross the ocean, too cold to handle.

CONTEXT AND BACKGROUND

Across the seas it's the Spanish Fleet ...
The Spanish dominated naval exploration
from 1492 to 1600, a period now known as
the *Age of Exploration*. Columbus's trip
inspired a number of sailor-explorers to chart
their own courses for "undiscovered" lands.
Spain, a wealthy nation with the world's
largest naval fleet, sponsored the majority of
these voyages. The important expeditions
are listed in Appendix I: Guide to the Age
of Exploration.

**Columbus named the country out of
error ...**
Thinking that he had arrived in India, Columbus
named the New World accordingly. The term
Indian wasn't derogatory when Columbus used
it. It was mistaken. The term is still used today,
though it also refers to "real" Indians (i.e. from
India). The Caribbean Islands are still called the
West Indies.

**1606, England sent John Smith to lead a
hundred colonists to Jamestown ...**
The English settlement in Jamestown was the
first successful colony in North America. John
Smith (a captain in the army) was not the leader
of the colony at this time but took a prominent
role later on.

   The men (there were no women) built a
large fort and met with the local Indians. But
they had made some crucial mistakes. The site
they had chosen was in fact a malarial swamp,
and a lot of them got sick and died. They had
arrived in May, too late to plant crops. When
the first winter came, many settlers starved,
froze, and died of sickness. Some men

★ PERSPECTIVES ★

If Columbus discovered it, why is it called America?

America is named after Amerigo Vespucci (pronounced Ves-pooch-ee), an Italian navigator who sailed for Spain and Portugal. Vespucci wasn't a captain like Columbus; he was a navigator on two or three much less important voyages to South America around 1500.

So why did Vespucci's name get on the maps? Some historians credit Vespucci as the first person to argue that the New World was not part of Asia but was a separate landmass. Others believe that it had more to do with Vespucci's famously outrageous accounts of the New World, which became best sellers in Europe. The books (which may have been forged) describe villages of sexy, giant women, strange love potions, voracious cannibals, and enormous clams brimming with hundreds of pearls. Clearly Vespucci, or whoever wrote the books, was making things up. But the stories captivated the imagination of Europeans, so Vespucci's books became more widely read in Europe than Columbus's own accounts.

When mapmaker **Martin Waldseemuller** was creating a map of the world in 1509, he decided to give the continent to Vespucci and wrote a note explaining: "I see no reason why we should not call it America, land of Amerigo ... man of sagacious wit." Waldseemuller later changed his mind and took "America" off his maps, but the word had gotten out and the name had stuck.

What the United States of America could easily have been named:

India

United States of Christopher

United States of Columbia

United States of Vespucci

We're coming overseas for more,
so Land Ho!

It was the year **1620**,
the **pilgrims** landed in the land of plenty,
sipping Henny. JK LOL BRB TTYL! :-)
Supplies shorter than Dora the Explorer.
Saw land calling "*Hoo-Ah!*"
like *Scent of a Woman*,
the Pilgrims had the sense
to bring some women,
'cause if you're fleeing to escape
religious persecution,
don't forget the LADIES!
All signed the **Mayflower Compact**,
except the LADIES!
But it was still progressive
and kind of crazy.
They split from the church;
they're breaking away,
while some folks in **Plymouth**
were just trying to get paid.
Probably would have died,
but **Squanto** helped them out,
brought them food, fur, and drink and
let them sleep in the house,
saved them. After **Thanksgiving**
he died of smallpox.
Are you picking up the pattern?
He died of smallpox!

I want America, I want America!
Crisscross the ocean, too cold to handle.

deserted to join the local Indians, who
were much more capable of dealing with the
cold winter.

Health became a problem and disease
would just devour the strength of the
manpower 'till it became the final hour ...
Two years later when reinforcements arrived,
more than 60 percent of the men were dead. It
was around this time that John Smith declared
himself the leader (essentially becoming a
military dictator). Smith had a hard-line motto:
You don't work, you don't eat. He also organized
work gangs and taught the men foraging
techniques that he had probably learned from
the Indians.

  Disney would have you believe that
Pocahontas and John Smith had a love affair in
the New World, but there is little factual
information to prove this. In any event, John
Smith was twenty-seven years old. Pocahontas
was eleven.

John Rolfe thought it'd be slick to make
money off of cancer sticks, dropping
tobacco off of his ships ...
Tobacco didn't exist in Europe before the
Spanish brought if back from the New World,
but it became an immediate hit. To capitalize on
this demand, Jamestown settler John Rolfe mixed
some mild Jamaican tobacco with a local
Virginian strain and began cultivating it in 1612. It
grew amazingly well. Tobacco exports to Europe
grew twentyfold from 1616 to 1619, soon
supporting the entire colony. Tobacco was
America's first *cash crop*—proof that the
colonies were financially viable.

Made Pocahontas his chick ...
Pocahontas was the daughter of the local
Indian chief, **Powhatan**. *Pocahontas* itself is a

nickname meaning "frisky." According to John Smith, Pocahontas had saved his life when Powhatan was going to have his head smashed in, but many historians now believe that Smith was actually undergoing a harmless initiation ceremony.

The colonists eventually kidnapped Pocahontas, and John Rolfe married her (supposedly in an effort to improve relations with Powhatan). Pocahontas was converted to Christianity and traveled to England with Rolfe and their son. Dressed like an aristocratic English woman, she was greeted with fanfare at the British royal court. Then she died of illness, probably smallpox.

In 1619 new force, government, set up the House of Burgesses . . .

In 1619 the colonists in Jamestown set up the House of Burgesses, the first representational government of the colonies. Though modest at first (its decisions could be overruled by the **Virginia Company**, which had paid for the voyage), it eventually became an influential political body. Also, 1619 was the year the first ship of African slaves arrived in the colonies.

It was the year 1620, the Pilgrims landed in the land of plenty . . .

In 1620, 102 colonists (women came this time) sailed across the Atlantic on a ship called the *Mayflower* and reached Plymouth in modern-day Massachusetts. Most of the settlers were **Separatists**, who wanted to separate from the Church of England. They were fleeing England to escape religious persecution. This group is now known as the *Pilgrims*. Others on the boat were looking for new life and for wealth.

All signed the Mayflower Compact, except the LADIES . . .

When the Pilgrims landed, they drafted the Mayflower Compact, a document that established **Plymouth Plantation** as a "civil body politic," under the sovereignty of King James I of England. Every man was required to sign it. More powerful in many ways than the House of Burgesses, the Mayflower Compact set up what some consider America's first true self-government (except for the self-governing Native Americans).

Probably would have died, but Squanto helped them out . . .

The Pilgrims arrived in Plymouth in December, and within months the harsh New England winter had killed half of them. Help came (as it had in Jamestown) from local Indians, especially one named Squanto, who apparently spoke English even before the Pilgrims arrived (historians are unsure how he managed this feat). Squanto and the local **Wampanoag** Indians taught the Pilgrims how to till the land, plant corn, and navigate the landscape—tasks that were instrumental to the survival of those first New England colonists.

After Thanksgiving he died of smallpox . . .

A successful harvest was literally the difference between life and death, and when the Pilgrims celebrated their first successful harvest, they invited some of the Wampanoag to thank them for their help and friendship. For three days the group feasted on turkey, venison, corn, and squash and took long naps. This was the first Thanksgiving. It was also around this time that Squanto died of smallpox or one of the other diseases that would ravage the Indian population in America.

We're coming overseas for more,
so Land Ho!

Britain was into **mercantilism**:
exported more than **imported**,
important for a system to enhance the
borders that they ship from.
Restrictions on colonial trade,
Navigation Acts
had the English getting paid off deals
that America made.
Not enforced every day, 'cause when
the good money would come,
Brits would turn the other way.
Salutary Neglect was OK,
nobody stepped in the way for that
Triangular Trade.
Colonies would barter rum for
African slaves
and send them back to
West Indian waves,
chopping down the fields of sugar cane,
harvested and shipped back
for the rum to be made
by **American slaves**
and **indentured servants**,
never to be paid.
Immigrants from Europe
dreaming of a better life;
in **1660**, you could own a man's rights.
Even in a time when we
outnumbered the whites,
you couldn't stand as a man and fight,
the future didn't seem bright.

I want America . . .
Religious and political oppression grew worse
in England during the first half of the
seventeenth century. A growing number of
British citizens, facing religious persecution at
home, decided to attempt the dangerous
journey to America. In 1628 a group of
Puritans struck a deal with the government,
under which they could set up a self-governing
colony north of Plymouth. These extremely
religious **Puritans** differed from Pilgrim
Separatists in that they didn't want to break
from the Church of England; they just wanted
to "purify" it. Roughly 1,000 Puritans made the
trip to Massachusetts in 1630, establishing the
Massachusetts Bay Colony.

**Britain was into mercantilism: exported
more than imported . . .**
Around 1650 Britain began to practice
mercantilism in international trade. The idea
of mercantilism is to export more than you
import in order to improve the economy.
To achieve this end, the British government
passed strict laws and tariffs protecting
the British economy and restricting
American trade.

**Navigation Acts had the English getting
paid off deals that America made . . .**
The English passed the Navigation Acts
between 1651 and 1673. These acts severely
restricted colonial trade, while benefiting the
English. The acts made it so that certain
American goods had to be shipped directly
to Britain, not to any other country. They
also dictated that only English or colonial
ships could carry cargo between
imperial ports.

Not enforced every day, 'cause when the good money would come, Brits would turn the other way. Salutary Neglect . . .

The colonies, for the most part, dealt with the Navigation Acts by ignoring them. They started smuggling, and England tended to look the other way. This developed into a policy of salutary neglect: the British often didn't enforce the laws that they had passed. In this case, the British probably realized that enforcing these acts would cause the colonies to rebel. Salutary neglect allowed them to keep the colonists happy and loyal.

Nobody stepped in the way for that Triangular Trade . . .

Both Britain and the colonies engaged in triangular trade, a system of lucrative international trade. Trade routes ran between the colonies, West Africa, and the West Indies. New England in particular got very rich from triangular trade. New England rum was shipped to Africa and traded for slaves. The slaves were taken to the West Indies and were traded for sugar and molasses. The sugar and molasses were then shipped to New England, where they would be distilled into rum.

American slaves and indentured servants, never to be paid . . .

Slavery was not immediately a huge Southern institution. Slavery was officially legal in the South in 1660. At that time, fewer than 1,000 slaves lived in the Southern colonies. As tobacco plantations grew in size, so did the use of slavery. Over the next decades, tens of thousands of slaves were taken from their homeland and shipped to America. By 1700, African slaves in the Southern colonies outnumbered free whites.

Slavery wasn't limited to the South by any means. Northern colonies kept Africans as slaves as well, and Northern ships got rich off of the slave trade. Most slavery in the North was focused in New York City. In 1703 nearly half of the households in New York City owned slaves.

In addition to slavery, the colonies employed a system of indentured servitude. Under this system, poor Europeans could secure passage to the colonies if they agreed to work for a number of years on a plantation. These indentured servants often worked for years in miserable conditions to secure their freedom.

AMERICA SPEAKS

"We must be knit together in this work as one man. We must entertain each other in brotherly affection. We must be willing to abridge our selves of our superfluities . . . We must delight in each other . . . rejoice together, mourn together, labor, and suffer together, always having before our eyes our commission and community . . . For we must consider that we shall be as a City upon a Hill, the eyes of all people are upon us . . ."

—John Winthrop, from his sermon "A Modell of Christian Charity", 1630

Winthrop is borrowing a phrase from Jesus's Sermon on the Mount to describe colonization in America as an important and spiritual undertaking. This phrase would later be used by many prominent figures including Abraham Lincoln, John F. Kennedy, and, famously, Ronald Reagan.

★★★ CHAPTER 3: ★★★

This Ain't Working

INTRO

Before George Washington was famous, back when he was a scrappy and serious young man, the governor of Virginia sent him into the wilderness to tell a group of French settlers that they were trespassing on Virginian land. The French greeted the young traveler, invited him in, and that night got so drunk on brandy that they let slip they had no intention whatsoever of leaving. The sober young Virginian headed back to his home and wrote a report of his adventure. He was then put in charge of a militia and sent back to the wilderness to force the French out.

The Minutemen

This was the beginning of the **French and Indian War**, which despite its name did not pit the French against the Indians, but instead the French *and* the Indians against Britain and the British colonies. In fact, this war was just another theater in the **Seven Years' War** (1756–63) that the French and British were fighting in Europe. In essence, the French and Indian War was fought over North American real estate. Who controlled the Ohio River valley and the area around the Great Lakes?

When the British won the war and negotiated the **Treaty of Paris (1763)**, the answer was clear: Britain gained control of all the land east of the Mississippi, including Canada.

But all wars are costly, and in the aftermath of the war, the British found themselves strangled in war debt. Nor were the members of the British Parliament thrilled about paying for a war that seemed to benefit only their colonies. So the British enacted a series of acts to tax the colonies.

The colonies clearly weren't happy with this arrangement and began protesting. But the British continued to tax the colonies and ignore colonial interests. The hotbed of dissent was New England. In 1770 after British soldiers killed five men for throwing rocks and snowballs in the **Boston Massacre**, colonists began organizing for violent resistance. At first, these rebels were merely fighting for their rights as British citizens. Eventually they were fighting to start their own country.

All was quiet like Ben Franklin's library ...

Ben Franklin opened the first public library in America. He also invented—

- bifocals
- the lightning rod
- the odometer
- a furnace called the Franklin stove
- the armonica (a glass harmonica)
- the catheter

and instituted—

- the fire department
- daylight savings time
- the political cartoon

CONTEXT AND BACKGROUND

And the British had a monopoly on selling tea, thanks to the Tea Acts ...
Three years after the **Boston Massacre**, Parliament passed the Tea Act of 1773, which gave the British a monopoly on selling tea to America by making the price so low that even smugglers couldn't compete.

Send a message to show George just where we at ...
Sam Adams and the radical **Sons of Liberty** were desperately looking for another Boston Massacre–type event to catalyze American resistance. The Tea Act provided just such an opportunity.

Dressed like Mohawk Indians ...
When three tea-laden cargo ships landed in Boston Harbor, Sam Adams led a group of 150 colonists dressed as Mohawk Indians to the docks. As a large crowd gathered to watch, the men boarded the ships and began to smash the crates and dump tea into the water. By the end of the night, the **Boston Tea Party** had destroyed $70,000 worth of British tea. It was a powerful message: like sticking a big middle finger across the Atlantic. King George of England took it to be just that. "The die is now cast," he told his prime minister. "The colonies must either submit or triumph."

Passed Intolerable Acts, but that don't phase me ...
The British responded quickly and fiercely. They passed the **Coercive Acts** and the **Quebec Act**, which together became known

This Ain't Working

LYRICS

It was a late dark night
in **Boston Harbor.**
Pitch black, while a fog hung
around the water.
This was the winter, **1773**,
and the British had
a **monopoly on selling tea**,
thanks to the **Tea Acts**,
but we're going to react,
send a message to show
George just where we at.
All was quiet like
Ben Franklin's library,
Then some people creepin' out of their
houses quietly.
Dressed like **Mohawk Indians**,
there were many men,
150 of them, all assemblin'.
A party gathered to check it,
like rubberneckers,
"Let's Twist Again," uh-huh,
like Chubby Checker.
Dressed up like Halloween,
Trick or Treat!
We're about to trick you,
George, we're going to dump your tea!
Sam Adams called out,
"Ya'll better follow me."
We dumped $70,000 worth of tea.
England didn't take it lightly,
uh-uh, they freaked,
'cause you know how the British just
love their tea.

Boston Tea Party

in the colonies as the Intolerable Acts. These
acts severely restricted democracy in
Massachusetts, closed Boston Harbor, and
even established Roman Catholicism as the
official religion in Quebec. The British also
sent 4,000 more soldiers into Boston to
suppress uprisings.

**Let me tell you the story of Paul
Revere . . .**
General Gage, the commander of the British
troops in Boston, heard rumors that the
colonists were amassing ammunition and guns in
a storehouse in Concord, a small town outside
of Boston. He also heard that two of the rebel
ringleaders— Sam Adams and John Hancock—

were hiding in nearby Lexington. Sam Adams had led the Boston Tea Party, and Hancock, the richest man in New England before the war, helped organize and fund the rebellion. Hancock later claimed his place in history by signing his name the largest on the Declaration of Independence. Gage planned to march out to Lexington and Concord, arrest Adams and Hancock, and then seize the ammunition.

But Paul Revere and the **Sons of Liberty** expected this move. Revere, a silversmith and maker of false teeth by day, set up a system of signals that would alert him if the British started to move.

One if by land, two if by sea . . .

In order to reach Lexington and Concord, the British had to cross the Charles River. Revere told a church deacon in Boston to watch troop movement and hang one lantern in the belfry if the British were coming by land, two lanterns if they were coming by sea. Revere and his horse were waiting on the other side of the Charles for the signal.

Two lights ignite . . . he and Dawes ride through the night . . .

Late at night on April 18, 1775, the deacon in Boston hung two lanterns from his church. Revere and another rider, **William Dawes**, saw the sign and sped off on horseback to warn the townspeople. They were later joined by a third rider, **Samuel Prescott**.

The British marched down into Lexington . . .

The colonies didn't have a standing army. Instead they relied on local militias and **Minutemen**, farmers who could grab a musket and assemble in a minute's time. Hearing Revere's call, a group of Minutemen

Passed **Intolerable Acts**,
but that don't phase me.
They're turkeys,
we'll smother them like we're gravy.
Sometimes you know I feel
like this thing we got ain't working.

Let me tell you the story of
Paul Revere.
He saved **John Hancock**'s career and
Sam Adams's beer.
It was the year **1775**, the Brits wanted
to steal some ammo and supplies.
At night Revere is like,
"Yo don't even fear,
just hang a lantern from the church
when they're coming near.
One if by land, two if by sea.
Then I'll speed off,
mad speedy through the country."
Midnight comes around,
Paul's getting antsy,
hands be twitching more than
Muhammad Ali's.
Two lights ignite, Paul's like "Oh yikes,"
hops on his ride, he and **Dawes** ride
through the night.
His voice in the darkness,
his knock at the door,
and his words that shall echo
forevermore:

assembled in Lexington to confront the
British. The British (also known as redcoats or
lobster-backs because of the bright red
uniforms they wore) were clearly superior in
training and numbers.

Captain said . . .
Captain Parker's actual words were, "Stand your
ground; don't fire unless fired upon, but if they
mean to have a war, let it begin here."
  No one knows who fired the first shot, but it
became known as the "shot heard 'round the
world" because of its far-reaching
consequences.

WHAT'S NEXT?

The Revolutionary War picked up quickly after the battles of Lexington and Concord with a series of battles that helped the rebel cause, including the **Battle of Bunker Hill**, in which the British took a heavy beating before winning the hill. The **Second Continental Congress** met in May 1775 in Philadelphia. Congress named **George Washington** from Virginia as commander in chief of the newly formed American Continental Army, which was really just a bunch of drunken farmers. Washington described the army as "excessively dirty."

In the next year, support for independence grew. This was due in part to **Thomas Paine**'s influential pamphlet called **Common Sense**, which argued persuasively for American independence.

* * *

AMERICA SPEAKS

"Is life so dear or peace so sweet as to be purchased at the price of chains and slavery? . . . I know not what course others may take, but as for me, give me liberty or give me death!"

—Patrick Henry to the House of Burgesses
upon returning from the First Continental Congress

"These are the times that try men's souls . . . Tyranny, like Hell, is not easily conquered."

—Thomas Paine in *The Crisis*, writing while Washington's men
were freezing to death at Valley Forge

**"The British are coming,
the British are coming!**
Kiss your youngins! Grab your guns!"

The British marched down into
Lexington,
and thanks to Paul Revere,
we were expecting them.
Captain said, "Don't fire unless you're
fired upon,
but if they mean to have a war,
we're going to bring it on!"
A shot rang out through
the morning.
The revolution was dawning,
it's daunting.
They killed us in Lexington,
moved on to **Concord**,
but we started putting medal on them
like they're honored.
We were ducking out of trees like
some Vietnamese,
dressed in brown
bringing **redcoats** to their knees.
They were all lined up
like in a soup line.
We polished them off
like they were shoe shine.

*Sometimes you know I feel
like this thing we got ain't working.*

**They killed us in Lexington, moved on to
Concord ...**
Somehow the rag-tag bunch of Lexington
Minutemen weren't able to kill even a single
British soldier, despite the fact that the British
lined up in a straight line to fire and were
wearing bright red coats. The British moved on
to Concord, expecting another easy battle. In
Concord, however, hundreds of Minutemen
took position behind stone walls, houses,
barns, and trees (in a kind of primitive
guerrilla-fighting style).

They were all lined up like in a soup line ...
The British were sitting ducks. Retreating to
Boston, the Redcoats took more fire from
Minutemen snipers hidden in trees and behind
houses. By the end of the first day of the
Revolutionary War, the British counted 73 dead,
and 174 wounded.

★★★ CHAPTER 4: ★★★
The Declaration of Independence (Interlude)

INTRO

The Second Continental Congress selected Thomas Jefferson to draft the Declaration of Independence. Jefferson was a statesman from Virginia who was known as an idealist and a good writer.

Jefferson locked himself in a room for a few days, writing on a special desk he had designed. In writing the document, he was heavily inspired by the ideas of the Enlightenment. The Enlightenment was a philosophical movement with origins in Europe in the seventeenth century. It proposed the revolutionary ideas that men were born with rights and that governments rested on the will of the people. For more information, see Appendix II: Guide to the Enlightenment.

John Hancock

The Declaration of Independence

TEXT

"When in the Course of human events it becomes necessary for one people to dissolve the political bands which have connected them with another and to assume among the powers of the earth, the separate and equal station to which the Laws of Nature and Nature's God entitle them, a decent respect to the opinions of mankind requires that they should declare the causes which impel them to the separation.

We hold these truths to be self-evident, that all men are created equal, that they are endowed by their Creator with certain unalienable Rights, that among these are Life, Liberty, and the pursuit of Happiness. (That to secure these rights, Governments are instituted among Men, deriving their just powers from the consent of the governed)."

CONTEXT AND BACKGROUND

Dissolve the political bands which have connected them with another ...
The colonies were breaking their relationship with Britain.

Separate and equal station to which the Laws of Nature and Nature's God entitle them ...
America was a colony, ruled by Britain, which was a country. The declaration stated that the United States should have the same status as Britain.

Jefferson believed firmly in God, but not necessarily the Judeo-Christian God. His religious views were shaped by the Enlightenment, which often merged God and Nature into one being.

A decent respect to the opinions of mankind requires that they should declare the causes ...
Or, in fewer words: "We don't have to write out all these reasons for splitting from you, England. We could just fight. But we're trying to do the right thing."

All men are created equal ...
The United States is the first government in the world to be founded on this amazing idea. Of course, it didn't seem to apply to the 500,000 slaves in America, or to women, or to Native Americans. Still, it represented a leap forward in political and moral thought.

To secure these rights, Governments are instituted among Men, deriving their just powers from the consent of the governed ...

The declaration stated forcefully that governments don't grant rights; they should protect peoples' rights. Furthermore, the government gets its power and legitimacy from the will of the people, not from God, tradition, or military power. These ideas come directly from **John Locke** and **Jean-Jacques Rousseau**.

WHAT'S NEXT?

That's just the beginning. What else does the declaration declare?

The Declaration of Independence is a declaration (we are the United States!) and a break-up letter. It basically says, "We're breaking up with you, King George, because you're a tyrant."

The declaration goes on to list "grievances" (all the things King George had done wrong). Here, instead of "you never bought me flowers" and "I never liked your haircut," it accuses King George of "cutting off [our] trade" and "imposing taxes on us without our consent." In all, it lists twenty-seven things that King George messed up.

The declaration ends by actually naming the new country: "We, therefore, the Representatives of the **United States of America** ... solemnly publish and declare, That these United Colonies are, and of Right ought to be Free and Independent States, that they are Absolved from all Allegiance to the British Crown."

Jefferson hates slavery?

Though a slaveholder himself, Jefferson's original draft of the Constitution blamed King George for the slave trade, which Jefferson called "execrable commerce." The delegates quickly deleted this passage, not only because most of them supported slavery, but also because blaming the slave trade on King George was totally false. Why Jefferson would criticize a system he supported (and that supported him) is unclear. It's typically written off as simple hypocrisy.

★ ★ ★

AMERICA SPEAKS

"What do we mean by the American Revolution?. . . The Revolution was in the minds and hearts of the people; a change in their religious sentiments, of their duties and obligations . . . This radical change in the principles, opinions, sentiments, and affections of the people was the real American Revolution."

—John Adams, Letter to H. Niles (February 13, 1818)

CHAPTER 5

It's the U.S. (Bust the A)

INTRO

The British have hundreds of warships floating by Staten Island, George Washington and his troops have been routed and chased out of Brooklyn and Manhattan, and soldiers are deserting en masse. Winter comes, and suddenly Washington realizes that many of his men don't even have shoes. After a series of humiliating defeats, Washington is on the run toward Philadelphia, the American capital, with thousands of British and German mercenaries on his tail.

There were some amazingly bleak moments during the American Revolution, during which very few held out hope for victory. But every humiliating defeat was soon followed by a triumph. After Washington was chased out of New York, he was able to sneak across the Delaware River

George Washington

under the cover of night on Christmas to defeat the British at Trenton. After the winter at Valley Forge, where Washington's men were freezing to death, America signed a treaty of alliance with France, which helped to turn the tide of the war.

As the war raged, America tried to form its first federal government. The first (more or less) leader of that first government was a man named John Hanson. The fact that you've never heard of him probably gives you an idea of how successful that first government was. It totally failed. But as the old saying goes: "If at first you don't succeed . . ."

LYRICS

We the People of the United States, in order to form a more perfect union, establish justice, insure domestic tranquility, provide for the common defense, promote the general welfare, and secure the blessings of liberty to ourselves and our posterity, do ordain and establish this constitution for the United States of America.

It's the U.S., bust that A and come back.
It's the U.S., bust that A and come back.
It's the U.S., bust that A and come back.
We do it like that, we do that.

Who's that? Working hard baby,
I'm not laid-back.
If you have money, better save that.
British want us to pay tax?
We'll lick your **Stamp Acts**!
We fought the revolution and won.
Time for states to form up like
Megatron. Some like "*aww naww*."
They liked **states' rights**, it stays nice.
Slave states get to keep their slave life.

Day one, drafted something to form
the nation:
Articles of Confederation.
It didn't have power
like **Masons**, so they're done.

★ FLOCAB SPITS FACTS ★ LIKE AN ALMANAC

• The U.S. Constitution has 4,440 words, making it the shortest Constitution in the world.
• The U.S. Constitution contains many spelling mistakes, including the glaring misspelling of "Pensylvania" just above the signers' names.
• Patrick Henry declined to attend the convention because he "smelt a rat."
• The original Constitution is secured in the National Archives in Washington, D.C. During the day, the document is displayed in a bulletproof case. At night, the Constitution descends deep into an underground vault, where it is locked behind five-ton doors built to withstand a nuclear explosion.
• At the convention, eighty-one-year-old Benjamin Franklin was too frail to walk. Instead, he had four prisoners from a local jail carry him into Independence Hall each day on a sedan chair.

★ BREAKDOWN ★

The Executive (the President):
- commands the armed forces
- approves or vetoes federal bills
- makes foreign treaties
- carries out federal laws
- appoints judges and cabinet members
- can veto laws

The Legislative (Congress, composed of the Senate and the House of Representatives):
- passes laws
- declares war
- can ratify or refuse to ratify treaties and appointments
- can impeach and remove the president or judges
- can override a presidential veto with two/thirds majority

The Judicial (the courts, the highest of which is the Supreme Court):
- interprets and applies the law by trying cases
- can declare laws unconstitutional

CONTEXT AND BACKGROUND

We fought the revolution and won . . .
Even before the Revolutionary War ended with the battle at **Yorktown** and the **Treaty of Paris of 1783**, the United States was trying to form a federal government. During the war, states acted independently, relying on their own governments and constitutions.

Some like *"aww naww."* They liked states' rights, it stays nice . . .
Most states were concerned that a federal government could grow too powerful and turn into a tyrannical regime such as that in Britain. Small states were concerned that their voice wouldn't be heard. And slave states were fearful that Northerners would use the federal government to control or even abolish slavery.

Articles of Confederation. It didn't have power . . .
The first try at forming a central government was the Articles of Confederation. The Articles established a virtually powerless central government. It had no executive branch, no judicial branch, no power to tax, no power to raise an army, no power to make treaties. It could only request taxes from states, not demand them. The country, meanwhile, was developing a huge wartime debt.

Farmer named Shay rebelled, caused trouble boys . . .
A postwar depression made life terrible for many Americans. Farmers across the colonies were beginning to echo the sentiment "the pursuit of happiness idea is great, but I'm starving over here." In 1786 a farmer named

It was too weak, like brittle bones
on bubble boys.
Farmer named **Shay rebelled**,
caused trouble boys.
A new **Constitution**,
that's the solution.
If you don't succeed,
you better try again.

It's the U.S., bust that A and come back.
It's the U.S., bust that A and come back.
It's the U.S., bust that A and come back.
We do it like that, we do it like that.

Don't put all your eggs in one basket.
Don't spoil your bag
with one bad apple.
Gimme a Break! Gimme a Break!
Break your government up
like a Kit-Kat Bar.
We hit it that far with our
checks and balances:
honestly a bigger deal than
sex and violence is.
Executive is **Presidential**.
He's essential,
doesn't make laws
just **signs** or **vetoes**.
Picks judges like **Sam Alito.**
Legislate law bringing heat though,
represent the people.
Two chambers like a shotty.
Senate kind of uppity, acting haughty.

Daniel Shay led 2,000 armed farmers through western Massachusetts, closing banks and courts. The federal government, however, could do nothing about it. With no army and no policing force, the government had to wait for militias in Massachusetts to suppress the uprising. **Shay's Rebellion** exposed the weakness of the Articles of Confederation.

A new Constitution, that's the solution . . .
A convention gathered in 1787 to address the weakness of the Articles of Confederation. Delegates included some big names: **George Washington**, **John Jay**, **Benjamin Franklin**, **Alexander Hamilton**, and **James Madison**. The first question became whether to try to amend the Articles or whether to trash them and start anew. The delegates decided to draft a new constitution, and the convention became known as the **Constitutional Convention**.

Don't put all your eggs in one basket . . .
The issues facing the writers of the Constitution all had to do with power: who has it and who doesn't. Needless to say, everyone wanted it.
The small states were concerned that their voices wouldn't be heard in a legislature, where the number of state representatives was determined by the state's population. New Jersey led this group with the **New Jersey Plan**, in which each state would send the same number of representatives. Big states like Virginia favored the **Virginia Plan,** which argued that the number of representatives in the legislature should be determined by population.
The delegates eventually settled on the **Connecticut Comprise**, which created a **bicameral** (two-chamber) legislature. In the Senate, each state would have two seats. In the House of Representatives, the state's population would determine the number of seats.

★ PERSPECTIVES ★

But what if later I want something different?

The United States Constitution isn't a perfect document. It was forged out of political compromises and battles. But its writers were wise enough to realize that they hadn't covered everything and that some things might eventually need to be changed. So they wrote into the Constitution itself a way to change the Constitution. As of today, we have amended the Constitution twenty-seven times.

Other ideas proposed at the Constitutional Convention

There were more than 600 highly contentious votes at the convention. Some of the delegates had conflicting views of the specific makeup of the republic. Alexander Hamilton wanted the president and senators to hold their posts for life. George Mason originally wanted there to be three presidents. One proposal argued that the presidency should be open only to people who were worth $100,000 or more (a multimillionaire in today's currency).

There was also a fight as to how to officially address the president. One proposal thought he should be addressed as, "His Highness the President of the United States of America and Protector of their Liberties." This was eventually passed over in favor of "President of the United States."

In the end, compromises prevailed. No term limits were set for elected officials (this was changed in the twenty-second constitutional amendment), but the president and congressmen had to run for reelection.

Democracy or Republic?

The terms democracy and republic have been used and abused for centuries. Technically speaking, the United States is a republic because its citizens do not vote directly on bills. Instead, the citizens elect representatives to do it for them. The word democracy doesn't even appear in the Constitution (neither does the word God).

True democracy is typically only found in small villages with "town-hall" meetings that allow everyone an equal vote. Still, many people call the United States a democracy, and many of the so-called republics, like the People's Republic of China, really aren't republics at all.

House of Reps is by population.
Big states send a congregation
all across the nation.
Judicial are the judges,
the dudes in robes.
What they wear under there
nobody knows.

It's the U.S., bust that A and come back.
It's the U.S., bust that A and come back.
It's the U.S., bust that A and come back.
We do it like that, we do it like that.

Don't spoil your bag with one bad apple ...
The second big debate was over slaves. The
Southern states wanted it all. They certainly
weren't going to let slaves vote, but they wanted
slaves to count toward their population (so they
could send more representatives to the House).
Ultimately the delegates agreed on a seemingly
random fraction: each slave would be counted
as **three-fifths** of a person.

**Break your government up like a Kit-
Kat Bar ...**
To guard against tyranny, the Constitution
organized the federal government into three
separate branches: **executive**, **legislative**, and
judicial. The members of each would be
chosen in different ways: executive by **Electoral
College**, legislative by popular vote, and judicial
by executive appointment. Furthermore, each
branch would wield different powers.

**Checks and balances: honestly a bigger
deal than sex and violence is ...**
The different powers of each branch were not
random. The constitutional delegates gave each
branch specific powers and limitations, so that the
three would "check" each other. In this case *check*
means the same thing it does in the line "you betta
check yaself before ya riggidy-wreck yaself." The idea
is that the three branches are checking each other's
powers, which creates a balanced government.

AMERICA SPEAKS

"Our new Constitution is now established and has an appearance
that promises permanency; but in this world nothing can be said to
be certain, except death and taxes."

—Benjamin Franklin, in a Letter to Jean-Baptiste Leroy (November 13, 1789)

CHAPTER 6

Bill of Rights

INTRO

The Constitution outlines the workings of the government but not the rights of citizens. Partly in order to get the Constitution ratified by the states, Congress made good on its promise to add amendments that would outline some of the rights of American citizens. The first ten amendments that were ratified became known as the Bill of Rights.

In general, these rights were both idealistic and, probably more important, reactions to English practices in the colonies. The founding fathers wanted to ensure that the citizens of the United States would never be victims of tyranny again.

The right to protest

Bill of Rights

LYRICS

Number One
Freedom of religion, speech, and press,
plus you can assemble in crowds
and protest.

Number Two
Right to bear arms and cannons,
I bet the Minutemen didn't know
about handguns.

Number Three
When soldiers gets sleepy,
you don't have to let them sleep
up on your couch.

Number Four
No one can search and seize.
It protects me, unless people
have a warrant to arrest me.

Number Five
If you arrest me, respect me.
Sorry, Alex, there's no *Double Jeopardy*.
What'd you do after school?
"I plead the fifth."
What'd you do after that, dude?
"I plead the fifth."
I don't have to incriminate myself
or risk my health,
whenever I'm in trouble,
I just plead the fifth.

CONTEXT AND BACKGROUND

First Amendment—Freedom of religion, freedom of speech, freedom of the press, and the right to assemble and petition.
Congress shall make no law respecting an establishment of religion, or prohibiting the free exercise thereof; or abridging the freedom of speech, or of the press; or the right of the people peaceably to assemble, and to petition the government for a redress of grievances.

There are, however, restrictions. The Supreme Court decided in 1919 that someone may not yell "fire" in a crowded theater just to be funny (*United States v. Schenck*). Nor, typically, can someone print something patently false about someone else (libel and slander), though these laws differ from state to state. States also regulate speech and press that are deemed obscene or pornographic.

Recent highly contested First Amendment rights issues include: the right of a judge to have a statue of the ten commandments in his or her courthouse, the constitutionality of saying the phrase "under God" in the Pledge of Allegiance, and the constitutionality of fenced-in *free speech zones*, where people are forced to remain to prevent them from causing disruptions during protests.

Second Amendment—The right to keep and bear arms.
A well-regulated militia, being necessary to the security of a free state, the right of the people to keep and bear arms, shall not be infringed.

The Second Amendment is the one touted by the National Rifle Association (NRA) and other gun-rights activists. But there is an enormous amount of debate surrounding the extent of this right and its consequences today. Certainly the founding fathers didn't know about handguns, which now claim between 7,000 and 14,000 deaths in the United States each year. The founding fathers did, however, know about British tyranny and Indian raids, both of which were fought with arms.

The writers of the Constitution believed firmly that the people must have both the ability to protect themselves and the power to purge the government of tyrants. As Thomas Jefferson said, "The strongest reason for the people to retain the right to bear arms is, as a last resort, to protect themselves against tyranny in government." But this argument faces modern-day complications. Back when the Second Amendment was written, the firearms used by the army and the firearms used by farmers were basically the same. The army may have had cannons, but the muskets of the Minutemen and the muskets of the British regulars were very similar, making it much more feasible to launch a revolution.

Staging a revolution today would be more difficult. Revolutionaries could amass a huge stockpile of handguns and assault rifles, but the federal government has billions and billions of dollars worth of planes, sophisticated rockets, tanks, bombs, battleships, and so forth, at its disposal. Some would consider Jefferson's original reasons for the Second Amendment no longer applicable. Others argue that the right of self-protection is the central idea of the Second Amendment and that guns are necessary for self-protection.

Third Amendment—Soldiers cannot be housed in private homes without the permission of the owner.

No soldier shall, in time of peace be quartered in any house, without the consent of the owner, nor in time of war, but in a manner to be prescribed by law.

This amendment is a direct reaction to the **British Quartering Acts**, which allowed British soldiers to stay in colonists' houses. The Third Amendment now seems rather out of place. It has never been the basis for a Supreme Court decision.

Fourth Amendment—Protects from unreasonable search and seizure.

The right of the people to be secure in their persons, houses, papers, and effects, against unreasonable searches and seizures, shall not be violated, and no warrants shall issue, but upon probable cause, supported by oath or affirmation, and particularly describing the place to be searched, and the persons or things to be seized.

Fifth Amendment—Secures due process of law for prosecuted individuals.

★ PERSPECTIVES ★

Jay-Z references the Fourth Amendment in the song "99 Problems." A police officer pulls Jay-Z over in his car and approaches him.

The cop says: "Well, do you mind if I look around the car a little bit?" Jay-Z replies: "Well, my glove compartment is locked, so is the trunk in the back, and I know my rights, so you're going to need a warrant for that."

That's the Fourth Amendment!

Number Six
You must process me speedily.

Number Seven
In front of my peers on the jury.

Number Eight
You can't use cruel
or unusual punishment.
You can't make me drink turpentine
for the fun of it.

Number Nine
The people get more than these rights.

Number Ten
States can make other laws,
and they just might.

This is the Bill of Rights.

Prohibits double jeopardy and self-incrimination.

No person shall be held to answer for a capital, or otherwise infamous crime, unless on a presentment or indictment of a grand jury, except in cases arising in the land or naval forces, or in the militia, when in actual service in time of war or public danger; nor shall any person be subject for the same offense to be twice put in jeopardy of life or limb; nor shall be compelled in any criminal case to be a witness against himself, nor be deprived of life, liberty, or property, without due process of law; nor shall private property be taken for public use, without just compensation.

This is the first in a series of amendments addressing the rights of citizens when facing prosecution. This amendment prohibits jailing individuals without charging them publicly with a crime. It forbids trying someone twice for the same crime (known as *double jeopardy*). Scholars and lawyers have also used the phrase "no person shall be . . . deprived of life, liberty, or property, without due process of law" as the basis for the idea that someone is innocent until proven guilty. The phrase "innocent until proven guilty," however, does not appear in the Constitution at all.

It also prohibits self-incrimination, putting the responsibility of proving guilt to the prosecution. This is where the famous phrase "I plead the fifth" comes from.

Sixth Amendment—The right to a speedy trial, the right to a lawyer, the right to call witnesses.

In all criminal prosecutions, the accused shall enjoy the right to a speedy and public trial, by an impartial jury of the state and district wherein the crime shall have been committed, which district shall have been previously ascertained by law, and to be informed of the nature and cause of the accusation; to be confronted with the witnesses

Seventh Amendment—The right to trial by jury.

In suits at common law, where the value in controversy shall exceed twenty dollars, the right of trial by jury shall be preserved, and no fact tried by a jury, shall be otherwise reexamined in any court of the United States, than according to the rules of the common law.

This protects against the will of a single judge by placing more power in the hands of the people. Interestingly, just like "innocent until proven guilty," the phrase "jury of one's peers" does not appear anywhere in the Constitution. There is great debate about to what extent juries ensure justice and to what extent they make their verdict based on personal prejudices and feelings. In general, however, it is thought that putting this power in the hands of the people is better than putting it in the hands of a single man or woman.

Eighth Amendment—Prohibits excessive bail and cruel and unusual punishment.

Excessive bail shall not be required, nor excessive fines imposed, nor cruel and unusual punishments inflicted.

Another important right for people facing prosecution; this amendment outlaws torture. The critical debate over the death penalty (used by the federal government and thirty-seven of the fifty states) often focuses on the Eighth Amendment: is killing someone a form of cruel and unusual punishment? In 1972 the Supreme Court prohibited the death penalty in the United States but then reinstated it in 1976. Today, America is one of the only industrialized nations in the world that still executes criminals.

against him; to have compulsory process for obtaining witnesses in his favor, and to have the assistance of counsel for his defense.

This amendment makes it illegal for the secret police to arrest someone without telling him the reason, whisk him off to Siberia, throw him in an underground cell, and have a "trial" for him that he cannot even attend. Many countries have performed these types of trials without justice. Some countries still engage in these practices today.

Ninth Amendment—Humans are born with rights; the Constitution does not give these rights to them.

The enumeration in the Constitution, of certain rights, shall not be construed to deny or disparage others retained by the people.

This was an important amendment for the idealists who wanted to make it very clear that humans have more rights than just those listed in the amendments. For example, the Constitution does not guarantee my right to eat, but that doesn't mean I don't have that right.

Tenth Amendment—Secures the power of the states.

The powers not delegated to the United States by the Constitution, nor prohibited by it to the states, are reserved to the states respectively, or to the people.

Essentially this amendment was included to assure states' rights advocates that states could set their own laws, as long as the laws didn't violate the Constitution.

★ ★ ★

AMERICA SPEAKS

"The framers of the Bill of Rights did not purport to 'create' rights. Rather, they designed the Bill of Rights to prohibit our government from infringing rights and liberties presumed to be preexisting."

—William J. Brennan Jr., Supreme Court Justice from 1956–90

INTRO

George Washington was unanimously elected to be first president of the United States. On April 30, 1789, he placed his hand on a Masonic Bible and took the oath of office. He even ad-libbed a little; he added the phrase "so help me God!" at the end, probably because he was so fired up to be the first president. Most presidents since have followed suit. Washington was a well-liked Revolutionary War hero who enjoyed long (seven-hour) fox hunts and puttering around his home, fixing things and gardening. When he came to New York to begin work as president (Washington D.C. wasn't built yet), he brought seven of his slaves with him.

Thomas Jefferson

The big beef in the United States during its infancy was between Hamilton (and his **Federalists**) and Jefferson (and his **Anti-Federalists**), both of whom were in Washington's cabinet. Jefferson was a states' rights supporter and opposed Hamilton's national bank. Hamilton thought Jefferson was idiotically idealistic. Jefferson thought Hamilton was a monarchist.

Jefferson resigned his vice presidency under Washington to form his Democratic-Republicans Party (known as **Republicans**) and won the presidency in 1800.

LYRICS

Yo, he step up in the **House**,
people call for joy,
but his slaves be thinking they're going
to jump this boy
for spitting all that **hypocrisy**,
talking about **equality**,
but beating brothers who ain't picking
up his cotton properly.
He wanted people to choose their
religion like dim sum.
Thought the Pres was too powerful
like King Kong.
Ding Dong!
Listen to this, not an **abolitionist**,
we're hitting this,
this is softball, slow-pitch. *Witch!*
Check the map, western
half is black and dark.
Buy Louisiana with bonds.
We're rich like Häagen-Dazs.
Jefferson sends out **Lewis and Clark**,
forty men, two-by-two like Noah's ark.
West on the Missouri,
winter in Bismarck,
this is nature dawg,
this ain't Central Park.
Indian teenager named **Sacagawea**
joins the group.
We're the Hekawi like F-troop.
Guides them through **Rockies**
like MapQuest,

CONTEXT AND BACKGROUND

For spitting all that hypocrisy, talking about equality, but beating brothers who ain't picking up his cotton properly ...
First, for the record, Jefferson never personally beat any of his slaves, but he did allow his overseer to do it, which some consider to be virtually the same thing.

Thomas Jefferson is probably the most controversial figure in American history. Some exalt him as the *Father of Freedom.* To others he was a slave-owning racist. Most people acknowledge that, like it or not, he was both.

Jefferson, who made the most forceful statement for general equality that the world had ever known (*We hold these truths to be self-evident, that all men are created equal*), owned 200 slaves throughout his life. Clearly he was not ready to extend equality to either blacks or women. Jefferson was an idealist, but his ideals were very much bound within the world he lived.

Jefferson himself may have said it best: "Bigotry is the disease of ignorance."

He wanted people to choose their religion like dim sum ...
Of the Founding Fathers, Jefferson was the most vocal supporter of the separation of church and state and of freedom of religion. Jefferson was often accused of being an atheist, probably because he thought that organized Christianity was a form of "tyranny over the mind of man."

Thought the Pres was too powerful like King Kong ...
Jefferson had always favored states' rights over the power of the federal government.

Remarkably, that didn't change when he became president.

One of the first things Jefferson did after taking office was to make the footprint of the federal government smaller. He cut taxes. He repealed tariffs. He repealed the **Whiskey Tax** that had led to the **Whiskey Rebellion**. He also cut military spending.

Buy Louisiana with bonds. We're rich like Häagen Dazs ...

The United States wasn't always a land "from sea to shining sea." The area west of the Mississippi, known as the Louisiana Territory, was owned by Spain and then France under **Napoleon**. Jefferson attempted to purchase the territory from Napoleon (he was scared that Napoleon, in his quest for world

domination, would try to build an empire in America). Napoleon needed cash and agreed to sell Louisiana to the United States for $15 million in April 1803. The United States agreed and the **Louisiana Purchase** nearly doubled its size. Ironically, the purchase was financed using bonds from Hamilton's **U.S. Bank**, which Jefferson had fought as unconstitutional.

Jefferson sends out Lewis and Clark ...

Jefferson hired Meriwether Lewis, a captain in the army, to head an expedition to map the newly purchased American West. Lewis chose his army buddy William Clark to co-lead the expedition, and the two of them hired forty skilled soldiers and hunters for the journey. One of the men also brought his slave, York.

Lewis and Clark set off from St. Louis in 1804. They were going "where no white man had ever gone before." In the Dakotas, they hired a French-Canadian trapper and one of his Indian wives, Sacagawea, as their guides. Sacagawea was an Indian woman. She was a teenager, and she was pregnant.

Indian teenager named Sacagawea joins the group ...

Sacagawea helped Lewis and Clark navigate the West. She acted as interpreter with some of the Indians (some of the Indians spoke English). She negotiated a crucial purchase of horses that the group needed to cross the Rockies. While on the trek, she also gave birth to a healthy child.

Expedition mapped the whole west ...

The Lewis and Clark expedition was an amazing success for the newly expanded United States. The group mapped a trail across the Great Plains, through the Rockies, and up to the Pacific Ocean. They made copious notes

met Indians and bears,
no time to nap or rest.
On the real,
expedition mapped the whole west.
Came home, Lewis killed himself,
he was depressed.
Who's going to mess with him?
He goes by Thomas Jefferson,
the dude who drafted
the independent declaration.
The tree of Liberty must be refreshed
from time to time,
with the blood of patriots and tyrants . . .

O.D.W.M.
O.D.W.M.
O.D.W.M.
We're talking 'bout some
Old Dead White Men.

There's a thin line between
a hater and a lover.
Burr and **Hamilton** running for
governor, but run for cover.
They're dueling. Hamilton missed the
mark like Crystal Pepsi,
Burr shot him in the face
like Dick Cheney.
What's amazing, kid, is what came after it:
Burr tried to form the United States
of Aaron Burr,
got caught, **tried for treason,**
gave many reasons,
washed his hands, jumped bail to

on the Natives, the rock formations, and the plant life. Unlike Columbus, Lewis and Clark were on a scientific journey—a true journey of discovery. They weren't looking for gold; they were discovering America.

They had only one fight with Indians, but no one was hurt. And they lost only one man to disease.

Who's going to mess with him? He goes by Thomas Jefferson . . .

Britain and France were both messing with America. To fund the expensive **Napoleonic Wars**, both the English and the French began seizing American ships. Tensions truly flared in 1807, when the British frigate **HMS *Leopard*** fired on the **USS *Chesapeake*** when her captain refused to let the British aboard. When the British finally did board the ship, they hanged four American sailors and sailed away.

Jefferson was outraged. He banned all British warships from American waters. Congress quickly passed the **Embargo Act** of 1807. The act prohibited any ships from sailing from a U.S. port to a foreign port, effectively ending all imports and exports. The act was designed to hurt the British and French economies, but it mostly hurt the United States.

Burr and Hamilton running for governor . . .

Although Aaron Burr was Jefferson's vice president, he was neither his friend nor his ally. This was back when presidents and vice presidents ran on separate tickets, unlike today when they run together and support each other. When the Republican Party dumped him from its ticket in 1804, Burr decided to run for governor of New York.

Alexander Hamilton, a longtime enemy of Burr's, wasn't actually running for governor himself. But he was totally determined to prevent Burr from ever getting elected. Hamilton called Burr a "dangerous man, and one who ought not to be trusted with reins of government." This and other attacks were totally successful, and Burr lost the race.

They're dueling ...
But Burr was hurt and wanted revenge. He decided to challenge Hamilton to a duel. Hamilton accepted the challenge to protect his honor. The two met on the cliffs of Weehawken, New Jersey, just across the river from New York City, at dawn. The pistols the men chose were smooth-bore pistols that were designed to be *less accurate* and thus make dueling less fatal. The sun, a deep orange, was just rising over the Atlantic. The two men assumed the dueling stance—their bodies positioned sideways to minimize the chance of getting hit. One of the witnesses called the start.

Hamilton missed the mark like Crystal Pepsi ...
Hamilton fired first, and missed. He may have missed intentionally. In his diary the night before, he wrote that he would "throw away" his first round.

Burr shot him in the face like Dick Cheney ...
Burr did not miss. He hit Hamilton in the hip (not the face), but the bullet entered his intestine, and the wound was deep. After thirty hours of extreme pain, Hamilton was dead. The vice president of the United States had shot and killed a man.

The only other time that a vice president would shoot a man while still in office was when Dick Cheney accidentally shot his friend in the face with a shotgun while hunting for quail in 2006.

Burr tried to form the United States of Aaron Burr ...
The amazing story really began after Burr shot and killed Hamilton. Burr met up with General James Wilkinson, who was in charge of the Louisiana Territory under Jefferson but was secretly getting paid off by Spain. Wilkinson and Burr decided that they would gather up some soldiers and ride into Mexico, where they would overthrow the government and form an **imperial dynasty**. Burr gathered roughly eighty troops and began the march through Mexico. But Wilkinson betrayed Burr and informed President Jefferson what his former vice president planned to do.

Jefferson quickly had Burr arrested and put him on trial for treason. Burr eventually jumped bail and escaped to France.

Jefferson and Sally Hemings sitting in a tree ...
The relationship between Thomas Jefferson and one of his slaves, Sally Hemings, has been a source of intense controversy for centuries. In Jefferson's own time, enemies picked up on this rumor and published stories, exposés, and poems in their newspapers.

In 1787, five years after the death of his wife, Martha, Jefferson was in Paris. His daughter Maria came to visit him and brought Sally Hemings, a sixteen-year-old slave from Monticello, Jefferson's estate. Some believe that this was the beginning of a thirty-eight-year relationship between "Tom and Sally," and that she bore him many children.

Most historians dismissed this story as a rumor, until DNA tests were done on Hemings's and Jefferson's descendants in 1998. The test proved (though not conclusively) that Jefferson and Hemings had at least one child together.

France. *Levez les mains.*
Jefferson's chilling in Paris,
thinking lofty thoughts,
one of his visiting slaves steals his heart.
She's dressed in yellow, she says "hello,
you probably noticed me
in the fields of Monticello."
Jefferson and **Sally Hemings** sitting in
a tree, M-A-K-I-N-G many babies.
First come scandal, then comes more.
Now Jefferson's got his face
on **Mount Rushmore.**

. . . Jefferson, Jackson,
Madison, Washington,
Monroe, Adams,
John Quincy Adams . . .

O.D.W.M.
O.D.W.M.
O.D.W.M.
We're talking 'bout some
Old Dead White Men.

Free Lemonade! Free OJ,
like Johnny Cochran.
Monroe Doctrine says Europe don't
come a-knocking.
Don't mess with our continent; we
ought to get a fence around
all of South America to keep you
people out of it.
Called it the **Era of Good Feelings**
but they're wrong.

**Monroe Doctrine says Europe don't
come a-knocking . . .**
The Americans entered the **War of 1812** in
reaction to the British practice of
impressment—forcing American sailors to
fight for the British. In general, America was tired
of the French, British, and Spanish maintaining
such a large military presence in (and in the
waters around) North and South America.
President James Monroe and his secretary of
state, John Quincy Adams, drafted the Monroe
Doctrine, which declared American dominance
in the Western Hemisphere and told Europe to
stay out.
   Ever since, American foreign policy has
reflected this doctrine, funding governments and
rebel groups in Latin America as it sees fit.

Called it the Era of Good Feelings . . .
After the battle of 1812, America experienced
a surge of patriotic fervor. The demise of the
Federalists allowed Republicans to enact all
the policies they wanted. This period of
relative political stability is known as the Era
of Good Feelings.

But they're wrong . . .
Women were second-class citizens with no
political voice whatsoever. The invention of the
cotton gin by Eli Whitney had made slavery even
more economically viable for white Southerners.
And Indians (like those led by **Tecumseh and
the Prophet** in Indiana) were routinely
defeated in battles over land.

Men getting richer than Enron . . .
The postwar boom helped the economy grow,
but the **Panic of 1819** (many state banks
folded) led to a three-year depression.

FLOCAB SPITS FACTS LIKE AN ALMANAC

In the War of 1812:

- The British Navy was capturing American ships and forcing American crew into its army. This was called impressment.
- President James Madison and Congress declared war against Britain.
- The war was fought in America, with naval battles in the Great Lakes.
- The British bombing of Baltimore inspired **"The Star-Spangled Banner."**
- The British invaded Washington D.C. and burned it. The president's mansion was painted white to cover up the fire damage, giving it the name, White House.
- **The Treaty of Ghent** (1814) ended the war, but the British in the Gulf Coast didn't get the news.
- The British invaded New Orleans and were totally repelled by **Andrew Jackson's** troops. The British lost 2,000 men. America lost 12. The victory propelled Jackson into the (newly painted) White House.

Andrew Jackson thinks he's a tough guy ...

Andrew Jackson was a cowboy general who was elected president. Unlike the Virginian aristocracy (Washington, Jefferson, Madison, and Monroe) and the rich Northerners (Hamilton and Adams), Jackson attempted to bring the voice of real America to the White House. The result was a renamed party (formerly the Republicans, now the **Democrats**), increased voter turnout, and a new frontier voice in American politics. Jackson's supporters even threw him a frat-style house party in the White House for his inauguration. More importantly, Jackson brought new powers to the presidency, using his veto power at will to shape national politics as he saw fit and setting the tone for powerful presidents to come.

Illegal wars in Florida, killing the Seminole ...

While Florida was still a Spanish territory, General Andrew Jackson led U.S. troops into Florida to fight the Seminole Indians in 1817. The invasion was prompted by Indian raids into Georgia and by the fact that a large group of runaway slaves had joined the Seminole. Since the war was waged on Spanish soil, it was technically illegal. When Florida became part of America, settlers and farmers wanted the land taken from the Seminole. The **Second Seminole War of 1935** was fought over Indian removal.

Putting the Creek in hellholes ...

In 1813 the **Red-Stick Creeks**, seeking to violently end white encroachment on their lands, attacked Fort Mims in Alabama, massacring the soldiers, women, and children. In response, Andrew Jackson and the Tennessee militia destroyed the Creek force in the **Battle of Horseshoe Bend**.

White men getting richer than Enron,
they're steppin' on
Indians, women, and blacks. Era of Good
Feelings doesn't cover the facts.

Andrew Jackson thinks he's a tough guy,
killing more Indians than there are stars
in the sky.
Illegal wars in **Florida**,
killing the **Seminole**.
Saying "hello" then putting the **Creek**
in hellholes.
Like Adolf Hitler, he had a Final Solution.
"Go away Indians! I don't want you
to live here anymore!"
Cherokee at the **Supreme Court**
appealed.
They got the boot, they had to walk
down the **Trail of Tears**.

O.D.W.M.
O.D.W.M.
O.D.W.M.
We're talking 'bout some
Old Dead White Men.

**"Go away Indians! I don't want you to
live here anymore!"**
Jackson wanted Native American lands for U.S.
settlers. Congress passed the **Indian Removal
Act** in 1830, giving Jackson the authority to
force Indians to move west using as much force
as necessary. The United States began forcing
the Cherokee to leave their homes in Georgia
to march west to Oklahoma.

**Cherokee at the Supreme Court
appealed ...**
The Cherokee Nation sent lawyers to the
Supreme Court to petition for their right to stay.
Chief Justice John Marshall ruled in favor of the
Cherokee and against their removal, declaring
them a "domestic dependant nation." Andrew
Jackson continued with the aggressive removal,
supposedly declaring, "John Marshall has made
his decision; now let him enforce it."

**They got the boot, they had to walk
down the Trail of Tears ...**
Between 1835 and 1838, the United States
forced the Cherokee on a long, dangerous
march across America, known as the *Trail of
Tears*. Nearly a quarter of the Cherokee
population died.

AMERICA SPEAKS

"A little rebellion now and then is a good thing ... God forbid we
should ever be twenty years without such a rebellion ... The tree of
Liberty must be refreshed from time to time with the blood of patriots
and tyrants."

—Thomas Jefferson, writing from Paris in response to Shay's Rebellion.

★★★ CHAPTER 8: ★★★
Frederick and Abraham (Interlude)

Anyone living in America during the 1800s could tell you the nation was divided. The division was between the North and the South. It could be traced geographically along the Mason-Dixon Line, which cut the nation in half. The division was chiefly because of slavery, but it was bigger than slavery. It was about power and economics.

Frederick Douglass

The North wanted more free states so they could control more elections. The South wanted more slave states for the same reason. Furthermore, wage-paying Northern businesses didn't like being forced to compete against slave labor in the South. Slavery supported not only the Southern economy but Southern society itself.

There were only a few voices in America at the time that dared to make slavery a moral question. Among them were Harriet Beecher Stowe, William Lloyd Garrison, and Frederick Douglass, all prominent abolitionists.

56

Frederick and Abraham (Interlude)

Frederick Douglass:

"Those who profess to favor freedom and yet depreciate agitation . . . want crops without plowing up the ground, they want rain without thunder and lightning, they want the ocean without the awful roar of its many waters. . . . Power concedes nothing without a demand. It never did, and it never will."

Abraham Lincoln:

"A house divided against itself cannot stand. I believe this government cannot endure permanently half slave and half free. I do not expect the Union to be dissolved—I do not expect the house to fall—but I do expect it will cease to be divided. It will become all one thing or all the other."

CONTEXT AND BACKGROUND

Frederick Douglass

The majority of slave owners in America prohibited their slaves from learning how to read or write, fearing that they could use these skills to escape oppression. One of the most extraordinary figures in history proved them right: Frederick Douglass, born a slave, would go on to become America's leading abolitionist.

After his amazing escape from slavery, Douglass settled in Massachusetts, where his improvised speeches on the evils of slavery caught the ear of local abolitionists. **William Lloyd Garrison**, a prominent New England abolitionist, hired Douglass to perform a series of speeches that propelled Douglass to celebrity status.

Douglass would go on to counsel Abraham Lincoln during the war, while recruiting African-American soldiers to fight for the Union. The quote on this track is an excerpt from Douglass's most famous speech.

Abraham Lincoln

As Jackson's Democratic Party grew in power and became the voice of the South, Northerners organized themselves to form the Republican Party, co-opting the name of Jefferson's old party. Nowadays it sounds weird to have Democrats winning the South and Republicans winning the North, but that just shows how the names of parties have shifted back and forth over the years.

With the tension between proslavery Democrats and mostly antislavery Republicans rising, the nation turned its attention to a Senate race in Illinois between Stephen Douglas and an unknown lawyer named Abraham Lincoln.

Lincoln ended up losing the seat to Douglas in 1858, but through a series of succinct and moving speeches, he captured the attention of America. The "house divided" speech is Lincoln's first famous speech. He compares the nation to a house: a simple but powerful metaphor. Two years later, in 1860, Lincoln would become president.

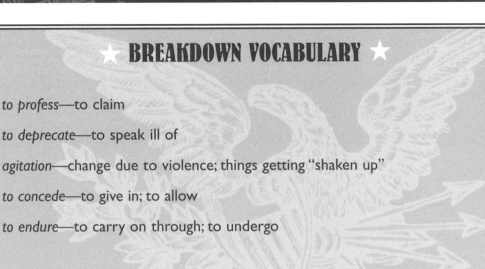

★ **BREAKDOWN VOCABULARY** ★

to profess—to claim

to deprecate—to speak ill of

agitation—change due to violence; things getting "shaken up"

to concede—to give in; to allow

to endure—to carry on through; to undergo

★ ★ ★

AMERICA SPEAKS

"I prayed for twenty years but received no answer until I prayed with my legs."

—Frederick Douglass

"America will never be destroyed from the outside. If we falter and lose our freedoms, it will be because we destroyed ourselves."

—Abraham Lincoln

CHAPTER 9

Ghosts of the Civil War

INTRO

Slavery and the economic and political differences between the North and the South were beginning to tear the country apart. The political compromises for determining if new states would be slave states or free states (**the Missouri Compromise**, and the **Compromise of 1850**) were beginning to fall apart as well. The South was thrown into fear and outrage after **Nat Turner's slave uprising** (1831) and **John Brown's raid on Harpers Ferry** (1859).

Nat Turner's capture

In the North, meanwhile, abolitionists kicked up their rhetoric. In 1851 **Harriet Beecher Stowe** wrote a novel called ***Uncle Tom's Cabin***. It was a long, melodramatic story about a slave family—basically a soap opera about escaping slaves. The amazing power of the book, though, was that it personalized the issue of slavery. The book was hugely popular, and it helped hundreds of thousands of Americans realize (for the first time) that African slaves were people too.

Ghosts of the Civil War

LYRICS

Nat Turner:
They call me Mr. Nat Turner,
I'm reppin' the South.
It's nothing to set a four-alarm blaze
to your house.
I'm being honest, my owner, Travis,
he treated us fair,
but I ain't nobody's slave. I'm getting out
of this here.
As God says, *so soon the first should be*
last, the last should be first.
I put my soul in the verse.
I saw blood upon cornstalks,
the sun eclipsed,
and it was time to get it cracking
like a thousand whips.
All out terror! Forty slaves on horses,
killing every pale face
and carrying torches.
My rebellion got squashed
in a few short days.
They executed me easy,
the South in a rage.
Nat Turner's gonna get you,
so please behave,
I'm a whisper in the wind,
I'm gonna rise from the grave.
In the South they went crazy by
lynching blacks.
I'm telling you the real, 'cause truth
should be a part of the facts.

CONTEXT AND BACKGROUND

They call me Mr. Nat Turner ...
In 1800 an African-born slave working in Virginia
gave birth to Nat Turner. Turner was both
keenly intelligent and deeply religious from a
very young age, often spending his time praying
and fasting.

My owner, Travis, he treated us fair, but I
ain't nobody's slave ...
Turner was bought and sold twice. After his
capture, he said his third owner, Joseph Travis,
"was to me a kind master, and placed the
greatest confidence in me; in fact, I had no cause
to complain of his treatment to me."

As God says ...
But by Turner's own account, God had bigger
things in store for him: "I heard a loud noise in
the heavens, and the Spirit instantly appeared to
me and said ... the time was fast approaching
when the first should be last and the last should
be first ... and I should arise and prepare myself
and slay my enemies with their own weapons."

I saw blood upon cornstalks, the sun
eclipsed ...
Furthermore, Turner began seeing signs that he
believed were from God: "While laboring in the
field, I discovered drops of blood on the corn, as
though it were dew from heaven." The same
year, Turner witnessed an eclipse of the sun. He
then began planning his uprising.

All out terror! Forty slaves on horses,
killing every pale face ...
At 2:00 in the morning on August 21, 1831,
Turner led a small group of slaves into his

master's house and murdered the entire family as they lay sleeping. Turner and his men then began marching house to house, murdering the white families and recruiting slaves. Turner's force eventually consisted of forty slaves, mostly on horseback. The group killed every white person they came across, fifty-five people in all.

My rebellion got squashed in a few short days . . .

Southern whites reacted quickly to the news, and local militias soon captured Turner and scattered his army.

John C. Calhoun

They executed me easy . . .

Nat Turner told his story to a local physician, who wrote it all down. The quotes above come from this document, *The Confessions of Nat Turner*. Turner was tried, hanged, and then skinned.

The South in a rage . . .

Nothing was scarier to white society in the South than a slave uprising. Turner's rebellion was a nightmare that had come true. The fact that Turner's revolt had been so bloody, so deadly (he had killed not only men, but women and children, too) seemed to justify slavery for many whites. More than ever, they clung to the belief that "if we let them free, they'll kill us all."

In the South they went crazy by lynching blacks . . .

The State of Virginia itself executed as many as fifty-five slaves suspected of being involved in the massacre, but the real violence took place outside the courtrooms and prisons. Angry lynch mobs became a regular sight in parts of the South. These mobs killed an estimated 200 African-American slaves.

Strict new slaves' laws passed in many states, including censorship of abolitionist materials, all with President Andrew Jackson's blessing.

I'm John C. Calhoun, and I love the South, the Senator from South Cakalak . . .

Though he died before the Civil War even began, John C. Calhoun was partly responsible for it. The Senator from South Carolina was the most powerful Southern voice in the government.

John C. Calhoun:

I'm John C. Calhoun,
and I love the South,
the Senator from South Cakalak,
reppin' the South.
They don't know me in the North,
but they try to play me,
states' rights best thing since grits 'n' gravy.
I believe firmly in the goodness
of slavery.
Northerners who hate it,
I think they have rabies.
Never before have Africans
been so civilized,
never before have they found the Lord,
Jesus Christ.
Northerners don't pay workers
enough to eat,
we don't pay slaves,
at least they have a place to sleep.
We must maintain the status quo for
whites and blacks
'cause if we ever let them free,
they're going to attack!
Dred Scott decision was right,
what belongs to me,
whether slave or mule, is my property.
We're chivalrous but don't mess with
us, **abolitionists,**
we'll cane you on the Senate floor.

We won't take no or maybe,
We're gonna end this slavery . . .

States' rights best thing since grits 'n' gravy . . .

Calhoun was Andrew Jackson's vice president, but he resigned after one term. Calhoun (ever the states' rights advocate) and Jackson (who was so pro-federal government that they called him "King Andrew") clashed over the **Nullification Crisis**.

In 1828 Congress had raised protective tariffs that helped the North but hurt farmers in the South. Calling it the **Tariff of Abominations**, Calhoun argued that his state, South Carolina, could nullify the tariff. Like Jefferson, he believed that states were sovereign. In response, Jackson got a less-strict tariff passed (the **Compromise of 1833**) as well as a **Force Bill** that allowed the army to march into South Carolina to enforce collection of the tariff. South Carolina backed down, but Calhoun's argument continued to inspire Southern thinkers.

I believe firmly in the goodness of slavery . . .

Calhoun was the leading proponent of slavery in the Senate. Previously, Southerners had argued that slavery was a "necessary evil." In a famous speech to the Senate, Calhoun took this much further, arguing that slavery was a "positive good."

Never before have Africans been so civilized . . .

Every pro-slavery argument is based in ignorance and racism, but none more than the argument that Africans were savages and that by living in America they were at least living in a civilized society. As Calhoun said, "Never before has the black race of Central Africa, from the dawn of history to the present day, attained a condition so civilized and so improved, not only physically, but morally and intellectually."

Harriet Tubman

Never before have they found the Lord, Jesus Christ . . .

Many pro-slavery arguments were based in Christianity. Why God or the Bible wanted Africans in particular to be slaves is unclear, but many Christians believed that they had the duty to spread the word of Christ to all of the world's people. Many whites also noted that the Bible supports slavery. In numerous biblical passages, slaves are urged to obey their masters. For a full list of Bible quotations supporting slavery, see Appendix III: Biblical References to Slavery.

Northerners don't pay workers enough to eat . . .

Calhoun and others noted with anger that while Northerners were yelling about the treatment of slaves, they were treating their workers worse than some slave owners treated their slaves. Indeed, young girls in textile mills in New England, for example, worked twelve-hour days under terrible conditions.

Dred Scott decision was right . . .

With the tension over slavery rising in America, President James Buchanan tried to avoid the issue by passing the buck. He said that the Supreme Court should settle the question of slavery in the territories. The case in question was **Dred Scott v. Sandford**, and it involved a man who had traveled the United States with his slave, Dred Scott. When the man died, Scott argued that because he had lived in territories where slavery was illegal, he should be legally free. The case went to the Supreme Court, where Chief Justice **Roger B. Taney** delivered the ruling that would shape the country.

Taney argued that Scott was a slave and slaves had no right to sue in federal courts. He

Harriet Tubman:

Children: I'm Harriet Tubman,
born into slavery.
In history I'm noted for my bravery.
I'm a runaway slave,
followed the **North Star,**
to take me from the South parts,
and I was never scared of the dark.
Like Dead Prez, boy, I'm an African,
more slaves down south, boy,
I'm going back for them.
Nineteen trips and not one a disaster,
like I told **Frederick,**
I never lost a passenger.
Reward for my capture: forty Gs.
Wanted posters all around saying
I can't read.
Still I slipped through the cracks
of that **Fugitive Slave Act,**
with so many freed,
I never lost my way back.
Jack-of-all-trades and you'd be surprised,
I was a cook, a nurse,
and even a spy for the North,
and this was during the Civil War.
Follow me while I'm following the
drinking gourd.
I did it all,
and it really wasn't a choice for me,
I only had two options, die or be free.

wrote that blacks "are so inferior that they had no rights which a white man was bound to respect." He went even further, noting that Scott was property, like a horse or a mule, and that slavery was fully supported by the Constitution.

This landmark decision was celebrated in the South, but it had another effect: many in the North who hadn't cared one way or another about slavery suddenly grew angry. The Republican Party was rejuvenated.

We'll cane you on the Senate floor . . .

Calhoun died in 1850 but his feisty spirit lived on in South Carolina. In 1856 Massachusetts senator Charles Sumner delivered a raucous antislavery speech in the Senate in which he attacked South Carolina senator Andrew Butler. He accused Butler of taking "a mistress . . . who, though ugly to others, is always lovely to him; though polluted in the sight of the world, is chaste in his sight——I mean, the harlot, Slavery!"

Representative Preston Brooks, also from South Carolina, decided to defend Butler's honor and entered the Senate that evening. He found Sumner doing some paperwork, snuck up behind him, and cracked him over the top of the head as hard as he could with the metal top of his cane. He continued to beat the senator, who was now bleeding profusely, for a minute or more.

In the ensuing days, both men became heroes in their respective regions.

Children: I'm Harriet Tubman . . .

Harriet Tubman was born a slave in Maryland around 1820. Like Frederick Douglass, she escaped to the North in 1849, but immediately returned to the South to help other slaves escape.

I'm a runaway slave . . .

Sneaking up through the South toward freedom was no easy task. Tubman used the **Underground Railroad**, which was neither a railroad nor actually underground. It was a loose network of individuals and houses sympathetic to the abolitionist cause. These families (many of them Quakers) would house the escaped slaves and send them on to the next "station," so that the slaves could gradually make their way north.

Nineteen trips and not one a disaster . . .

Amazingly, Tubman risked her life nineteen times by returning to the South to help more slaves escape. She ultimately helped 300 slaves find their freedom, and she didn't lose a single person.

Reward for my capture: forty Gs . . .

The South knew about Harriet Tubman and also knew that she was more dangerous as a symbol than as a slave-runner. At one point the reward for her capture was $40,000.

I slipped through the cracks of that Fugitive Slave Act . . .

The Fugitive Slave Act, which passed through Congress as part of the **Compromise of 1850**, required citizens of any state, slave or free, to assist in the capture and return of runaway slaves.

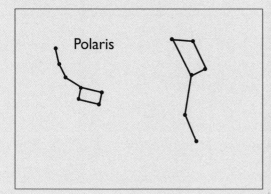

Polaris

I was a cook, a nurse, and even a spy for the North. . .

Tubman served for the Union during the Civil War, working as a spy behind Confederate lines, a nurse, and a cook. At one point during the war, she and a group of Union troops reportedly led 750 slaves to freedom.

Follow me while I'm following the drinking gourd . . .

Tubman and other escaped slaves moved at night, using the stars as their guides, especially Polaris, the North Star. Many slaves taught each other to locate Polaris by using the stars of the Big Dipper (aka the drinking gourd).

I'm Abraham Lincoln . . .

Abraham Lincoln was born in 1809 in Kentucky, the son of an illiterate pioneer farmer. He later moved to Illinois, where he became a lawyer.

I'm from Illinois . . .

Lincoln had been a mostly unsuccessful politician until 1860, when he ran for president. The newly powerful Northern Republicans, however, organized behind the tall, impressive man from Illinois and he won the presidency without carrying a single Southern state (in ten slave states he didn't even receive a single popular vote).

North rich like cha-ching . . .

As potential war approached, it seemed it would be an easy victory for the North, which had more than twice the polulation, twice the miles of railroad, five times the factories, ten times the workers, and nearly five times the money ($189 million dollars in bank deposits). All the South had going for it were better generals, knowledge of the land, and that famous rebel yell.

Abraham Lincoln:

I'm Abraham Lincoln, what y'all thinking?
I'm from **Illinois**, you illin' boy,
North rich like cha-ching.
All slave states think that they're going
to **secede**?
Like the **Fugitive Slave Act**,
running away ain't easy.
A house divided against itself
cannot stand,
like **Betsy Ross** trying to climb on
Uncle Sam's hands.
I said I wasn't gonna mess
with your slavery,
but the South didn't buy it,
they were hating me.
I switched reasons to fight
from **Union** to slavery
like Bush, Iraq's empty of WMDs.
Emancipation Proclamation
made France like me.
Who needs friends, Jefferson Davis?
You have me as an enemy.
Who do you have?
Stonewall Jackson and
Robert E. Lee?
I've got **U. S. Grant** and
Sherman's March to the Sea.
I wanted to be soft on the
Confederacy like Huggies,
but after **Booth** shot me,
nobody wanted to hug me . . .

We won't take no or maybe,
We're gonna end this slavery . . .

Slave states think that they're going to secede . . .
A month after Lincoln's victory, South Carolina voted to secede from the United States of America. Two months later, six more states did the same. These governments joined together to form the **Confederate States of America**. They elected Jefferson Davis as the Confederacy's first president. After Lincoln gathered an army, three more states joined the Confederacy. Three slaves states remained loyal to the Union.

I said I wasn't gonna mess with your slavery, but the South didn't buy it . . .
Southern states left the Union in spite of the fact that Lincoln had promised that he would not interfere with slavery in the South. He said, however, that he would forbid slavery in new territories.

I switched reasons to fight from Union to slavery . . .
The Civil War was fought to keep the Union together. Only later did Lincoln (and public perception) make it a war about ending slavery. Lincoln was a politician, and he was very aware that most Northerners wouldn't fight to emancipate slaves. However, they would fight to keep America united.

With the **Emancipation Proclamation** (1863), Lincoln added a new objective of the war: abolishing slavery.

Bush, Iraq's empty of WMDs . . .
Lincoln never dropped saving the Union as the Civil War's primary objective, so the comparison falls short, but it is worthwhile to note that when George W. Bush switched the reason for the war in Iraq from finding and destroying weapons of mass destruction (there were none)

to regime change, he was not the first president to alter or add to the reasons for a war while already halfway through it.

Emancipation Proclamation made France like me . . .

Lincoln issued his Emancipation Proclamation not to free all slaves (it didn't, just those in the Confederacy), but to drum up European support for the Union and to help destroy the Southern economy. It proved a brilliant political move as Britain and France soon pledged their support.

Who needs friends, Jefferson Davis? . . .

Jefferson Davis was actually an opponent of secession before the Confederacy nominated him president. As the leader of the Confederacy, he failed to appoint a general-in-chief to coordinate strategy until late in the war. Instead, Jefferson chose to defend each part of the South equally, a strategy that some argue cost the Confederacy the war.

Who do you have? Stonewall Jackson and Robert E. Lee?

The most important man of the Confederacy was Robert E. Lee, the brilliant general who won a series of battles in which his troops were vastly outnumbered.

Stonewall Jackson was a leader of Confederate troops under Lee, who was best known for leading a brilliant flanking move against the Union in the **Battle of Chancellorville**. The battle ended poorly for Jackson himself, though. Returning to camp, he was accidently shot by a Confederate soldier and died soon after.

I've got U. S. Grant and Sherman's March to the Sea . . .

The Union had a series of inept generals who failed to win battles and failed to follow Lincoln's orders. Exceptions were General **Ulysses S. Grant**, who led successful offensives at **Vicksburg** and along the Mississippi River, and

General **William Tecumseh Sherman** (named at birth after the notorious Indian chief), whose famous March to the Sea across Georgia and through Atlanta ravaged and destroyed the land. As Sherman himself noted, "we devoured the land."

I wanted to be soft on the Confederacy like Huggies . . .

After the war, Lincoln outlined a policy for letting Southern states back into the Union that was generous and compassionate. Many members of his Republican Party thought these policies were too generous and didn't punish the South enough for the enormously costly Civil War. Lincoln, however, never got a chance to put these plans in place.

But after Booth shot me, nobody wanted to hug me . . .

Lincoln was shot and killed by an actor, John Wilkes Booth, a Confederate sympathizer, while watching a comedy at Ford's Theatre on April 14, 1865. American reconstruction was left to Lincoln's successor, **Andrew Johnson.** Johnson's moderate approach to reconciliation clashed with radical Republicans from the North, leading to his impeachment.

AMERICA SPEAKS

"I am quite certain that the crimes of this guilty land will never be purged away but with blood."

—John Brown, speaking at his execution. Brown had led a group of abolitionist followers in an attack on a federal arsenal at Harpers Ferry in 1859. Harriet Tubman had planned to join Brown's uprising, but she fell ill a few days before.

"My paramount object in this struggle is to save the Union, and is not either to save or to destroy slavery. If I could save the Union without freeing any slave I would do it, and if I could save it by freeing all the slaves I would do it."

—Abraham Lincoln, in his Letter to Horace Greeley (August 22, 1862)

★★★ CHAPTER 10: ★★★
Big Ballin'
(in the Gilded Age)

INTRO

Northern Republicans hated Andrew Johnson. Johnson had succeeded Lincoln as president and now had to deal with the **Reconstruction**. But his "go easy on the Confederacy" policies and his total lack of commitment to rights for former slaves put him at odds with the radical Republicans in Congress. The South was passing laws designed to make free blacks into virtual slaves, and Johnson nodded along.

In response, Congress passed the **Fourteenth Amendment** in 1866, which states that all persons born or naturalized in the United States are citizens and are entitled to equal protection and due process of law. The Congress then **impeached** Johnson on a technicality, but he was acquitted. (*Impeachment* does not mean that the president is removed from office, only that he is *tried* for impeachment. Bill Clinton was the only other president ever to be impeached.)

After Reconstruction, America went back to doing what it does best: making money. It was the era of big business. While corruption plagued the government, money-hungry entrepreneurs took advantage of the government's lax economic policies and formed huge corporations. These powerful men, most notably John D. Rockefeller, Andrew Carnegie, and J. P. Morgan, used their businesses to squash competition and control the market. For two decades, they truly ruled America.

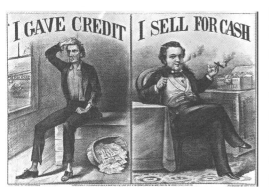

Big Ballin' (in the Gilded Age)

LYRICS

John D. Rockefeller:
I don't even need a beat.
I could kick it a cappella.
Doo-wop, shoo-wop.
I'm John D. Rockefeller.
I'm bigger than *Big Pimpin'*,
I'm bigger than Jay-Z.
He named his record company after me.
I'm the O.G. with more oil than *Valdez*.
Standard Oil?
That's just one of my companies.
I formed the **trust**, yes I did.
Now I'll gobble up these Colonel
Sanders like they're chicken feed, see?

J. P. Morgan:
Who's next? That'd be me, J. P. Morgan,
vital organ, fire people
like they're orphans.
Yeah, you heard about me,
Age is Gilded. Banks: I built it.
Towns: I filled it.
This **robber baron** is hotter than
most of these wack cats,
I'm a real hustler putting
trains on rail tracks.
Kicking those real facts,
little homey pay attention:
the only one to use the law
to bring me my position.

CONTEXT AND BACKGROUND

I could kick it a cappella. Doo-wop, shoo-wop. I'm John D. Rockefeller . . .
John D. Rockefeller was a young bookkeeper when his bosses told him to report on whether or not oil was a good investment. He lied and told them it had "no future." Then he went on to form what would become the biggest oil company in the United States.

I'm the O.G. with more oil than *Valdez*. Standard Oil . . .
Rockefeller's **Standard Oil Company** completely dominated the booming oil market. Based in Cleveland, Ohio, Standard Oil grew and grew by buying out smaller rivals. Standard Oil also reportedly attacked rival companies using bribery, sabotage, and secret deals with railroads.

I formed the trust, yes I did . . .
While the government was very hands-off with the economy, there were still some laws in place governing corporations. To bypass these restrictions, Rockefeller (and his attorney Samuel Dodd) invented the trust, a giant organization of big businesses under one umbrella.

Now I'll gobble up these Colonel Sanders like they're chicken feed . . .
As soon as Standard Oil became a trust, it could legally own virtually the entire oil industry. Rockefeller quickly gobbled up all of his competitors, forming a giant monopoly. By 1879 Rockefeller controlled more than 90 percent of the nation's oil refineries.

Who's next? That'd be me, J. P. Morgan . . .
J. P. Morgan first made a name for himself

during the Civil War, not as a hero (he dodged the draft by paying $300), but as a moneymaker. He bought rifles from the government, refitted them, and then sold them back to the government for a huge profit.

Morgan was a banker, and after the war he expanded his banking empire to colossal proportions. His bank houses were so large they loaned money to other banks. Morgan also got into the railroad business.

Yeah, you heard about me, Age is Gilded ...

The era of big business is also known as the **Gilded Age**. The word *gilded* means gold-plated (but cheap on the inside). This era is called the Gilded Age because a handful of tycoons were getting insanely rich, but the booming economy hid corruption, dirty-deals, and the working poor that lay below the surface of society. The tycoons themselves were called *robber barons*.

I'm a real hustler putting trains on rail tracks ...

Jay Gould and **Cornelius Vanderbilt** were the original railroad tycoons following the Civil War, but their empire mostly collapsed after the **Black Friday** stock market crash of 1869. In the 1890s, J. P. Morgan stepped into the promising railroad industry. He and his friends began buying up huge amounts of America's railroad. By 1900 Morgan himself owned half of America's track mileage, and his friends owned most of the rest, allowing them to set prices and control trade.

Carnegie Steel, yeah we have a whole monopoly ...

Andrew Carnegie was the steel tycoon. His company, **Carnegie Steel**, dominated steel production in the United States. In 1900

Carnegie teamed up with J. P. Morgan to create U.S. Steel, the first billion-dollar corporation.

Like Horatio Alger, I'm rags to riches ...

Unlike other robber barons, Carnegie was born poor. He emigrated from Scotland with his family and worked in a cotton factory before working his way to the top of the steel empire.

Horatio Alger was an author who wrote fictional tales of American boys going from "rags to riches." These popular books helped create an idea of the **Gospel of Success**: anyone could become rich and famous in America if he or she had enough ambition and perseverance.

Social Darwinism, yeah, I can't be stopped ...

Darwin's extremely important theory of evolution argued that human beings had evolved from more primitive life-forms. Evolution depended on **"survival of the fittest":** only the strongest and most adaptable animals survive to pass on their genes.

Andrew Carnegie took this idea and applied it to economics and society. In his 1889 essay, "**The Gospel of Wealth**," Carnegie argued that free-market economics would allow the strongest companies to survive, and that the smartest, most hardworking people would rise to the top of society. This idea was called social Darwinism, and Carnegie and others used it to justify the enormous gap between the rich and the poor.

The U.S. government needed money, asking for help ...

In 1895 the U.S. government was running out of gold, so it actually turned to one of its citizens to bail it out. J. P. Morgan gave the government $62 million in gold in exchange for U.S. bonds. He then sold the bonds for enormous profit.

LYRICS. continued

Andrew Carnegie:

Pass the mic, I'm Andrew Carnegie,
the one all these U.S. senators
want to be.
The opposite of poverty,
Carnegie Steel,
yeah we have a whole **monopoly**.
Like **Horatio Alger**, I'm rags to riches.
I used to have no dough,
now my paper's vicious.
Social Darwinism, yeah,
I can't be stopped,
like that metal after it pop, I'm h-h-hot ...

I'm the boss, I'm livin' large,
I'm a tycoon, and I'm big ballin'...

J. P. Morgan:

Yeah, you know who it be ... J. P.,
Morgan that is. ...
Here's the situation:
the U.S. government needed money,
asking for help,
now something here sounds funny.
My mamma said good deeds
don't ever come back,
so they hit me with
Sherman Antitrust Act.
It's got to be a gimmick,
you saying if I'm too rich,
they make a law to tell me
how I've got to spend it?
The **laissez-faire economy** saved me.

They hit me with the Sherman Antitrust Act ...

Realizing that things were getting out of hand, Congress began attempting to regulate these giant trusts. In 1888 Congress passed the **Interstate Commerce Act** to try to stop price-fixing on the railroads. In 1890 Congress passed the Sherman Antitrust Act, which outlawed trusts. But big business wasn't so easily stopped. These acts were rarely enforced. In fact, lawyers for big business began using the Sherman Antitrust against striking unions. So while Congress was trying (meekly) to regulate trade, the courts were clearly pro-business.

The laissez-faire economy saved me ...

Following the Civil War, the government practiced a hands-off policy toward business. The government believed in a laissez-faire economy (*laissez-faire* is French for "let be"). The idea is that a free economy will regulate itself and that competition will create fair wages and prices. The government didn't realize that the robber barons would literally stomp out competition.

I'm Jo Pulitzer. I'm 10 on the Richter ...

At the opening of the twentieth century, two more men emerged as extremely influential power brokers. **William Randolph Hearst** and Joseph Pulitzer owned newspapers, and they used their newspapers to control the views of American citizens.

U.S. goes to war, I use news to divide us ...

Pulitzer and Hearst learned during the Civil War that blood and war sold newspapers. Years later, both men began using their newspapers to push America toward war. In Cuba, nationalists had been rebelling against Spanish rule, so Pulitzer and Hearst began exaggerating and even inventing accounts of Spanish atrocities to sell more papers. Soon the American public was clamoring for action against Spain.

In Cuba, Teddy Roosevelt's screaming *Rough Riders!* ...

The Spanish-American War (1898) lasted only two months. The U.S. invaded **Cuba** and the **Philippines** and conquered both. Eager for war heroes, Pulitzer and Hearst sent war correspondents to follow **Theodore Roosevelt,** who was leading a volunteer cavalry known as the Rough Riders through Cuba. Teddy Roosevelt and the Rough Riders become famous after their victory on **San Juan Hill.**

I don't need no facts, this is yellow journalism. Exaggerate the truth, Sensationalism ...

The journalistic practices of these newspapers are called *yellow journalism* and *sensationalism*. Actual facts didn't matter much. The newspapers printed almost anything in an effort to sell more papers and influence their readers.

I keep the prices high, the wages low, so the Knights of Columbus know who's in control ...

Controlling an entire industry meant having no competition. Having no competition allowed the robber barons to set prices extremely high, while keeping the wages they paid their workers very low.

The workers weren't entirely silent during this period. Hazardous working conditions, low pay, and long hours led hundreds of thousands of workers to organize into unions. The Knights of Columbus were one of the first major unions. They demanded equal pay for women and an end to child labor, among other progressive ideas. In 1885 the Knights of Columbus led a successful strike against **Jay Gould's** railroad company. A year later, however, violence and death at the **Haymarket Riot** in Chicago caused the union to fold.

These machine politics are getting kind of sleazy ...

During the Gilded Age, the power of the vote wasn't in the hands of individuals. It was in the hands of political machines: local organizations that distributed jobs, city contracts, and other benefits in exchange for votes. These **machine politics** were dominated by party bosses who acted a lot like mob bosses, thriving off of power and corruption.

Me and Boss Tweed, yeah we own the vote, Tammany Hall, playa ...

The most powerful local boss in America was William Marcy Tweed. Boss Tweed was, in many ways, the king of New York, and Tammany Hall was his court. Through a mixture of favors and intimidation, Tweed controlled the vote, and by owning the vote, he owned the legislators. So Boss Tweed essentially controlled legislation in New York without even holding an elected position.

★ PERSPECTIVES ★

Pulitzer—how they set the standard for all prize winners ...

The Pulitzer Prize is now one of the world's most revered and distinguished honors. Each year a committee awards the prize to notable authors, photographers, musicians, and journalists for specific works. Ironically, the prize was founded by Pulitzer (in his will), who wasn't exactly known for truthful reporting in his newspapers.

LYRICS, continued

The rest can't touch 'cause I'm higher
than Marley.

Jo Pulitzer:
I'm Jo Pulitzer. I'm 10 on the Richter.
I'm how they set the standard
for all prize winners.
U.S. goes to war, I use news to divide us.
In Cuba, **Teddy Roosevelt's**
screaming **Rough Riders!**
So tell me who's in control
of your worldview.
The man with paper in hand,
Pulitzer's the truth.
I don't need no facts,
this is **yellow journalism.**
Exaggerate the truth, **Sensationalism.**

John D. Rockefeller:
Rockefeller eats shrimp dipped in caviar,
I don't need a car, I ride on real jaguars.

I keep the prices high, the wages low,
so the **Knights of Columbus** know
who's in control.
I own 90 percent of oil, keep it greasy.
These **machine politics** are getting
kind of sleazy.
Me and **Boss Tweed**,
yeah we own the vote,
Tammany Hall, playa. That ain't no joke!

I'm the boss, I'm livin' large,
I'm a tycoon, and I'm big ballin'...

WHAT'S NEXT?

In the early twentieth century, a
backlash against the corruption and
excesses of the Gilded Age took hold in
Washington and across the nation.
Congress launched a series of
economic, social, and environmental
reforms in what is now known as the
Progressive Era.

Journalistic practices flipped 180
degrees after the Spanish-American War.
A new breed of journalists were called
muckrakers because they dug up dirt
in search of corruption.

Theodore Roosevelt became the first
president in many years who wasn't
pro-business. Roosevelt strengthened
the Sherman Antitrust Act and
promised Americans a **Square Deal**:
no one group would be favored
over others.

Roosevelt also believed that the
United States should dominate Latin
America. He basically created a nation,
Panama, just so that the United
States could dig and own the
lucrative **Panama Canal**, the only
water passage through Central
America linking the Atlantic and
Pacific oceans.

Feminism also grew in power. Led by
Susan B. Anthony, women suffragists
held rallies and picketed the White

House. Their voices finally too loud to ignore, the **Nineteenth Amendment** passed in 1920, granting women the right to vote.

World War I in a Nutshell
The cheese sandwich that started it all . . .
In 1914 a group of young students in Sarajevo decided to kill the heir to the throne of the Austro-Hungarian Empire, Archduke Franz Ferdinand. The students were Bosnian-Serbs, and they wanted Bosnia to join independent Serbia to the south. So they plotted to kill Ferdinand on June 28, when the archduke would be traveling through the city. But these students were inexperienced, and their plot immediately began falling apart.

The first assassin couldn't get a shot off. The second threw a bomb, but it hit the wrong car; he then threw himself in a river, but it was only four inches deep, so a mob pulled him out and beat him. Most of the other assassins fled, and the motorcade sped away.

It had been a crazy morning: the archduke had nearly been killed, and had just nearly escaped to safety. But the story doesn't end there. One of the wannabe assassins, convinced that his plot had failed, wandered into a sandwich shop to get something to eat. He bought a cheese sandwich and sat in the window, gazing at the Sarajevo streets and feeling dejected.

But just then, Ferdinand's car came driving by. Ferdinand had decided to go to the hospital to visit one of the bomb-attack victims. But his car took a wrong turn and ended up in a dead-end alley right in front of the sandwich shop.

The assassin saw the car, dropped the sandwich, ran out of the shop, and shot and killed Franz Ferdinand, thus starting World War I.

Originally known as the Great War, World War I was really caused by growing tensions between the empires and nations in Europe. The **Central Powers** (Germany, Austria-Hungary, and the Ottoman Empire) fought the **Allied Powers** (Britain, France, Russia, and later the United States) in what would prove to be a bloody nightmare for the world. The war pitted old technology against new with men on horses riding against machine guns and soldiers using bayonets while giant fleets of submarines controlled the seas.

Initially, America was very happy not to be involved in such a destructive war, but eventually national sentiment changed. German submarines began sinking American ships with greater frequency, including the famous **Lusitania**. America intercepted the **Zimmerman Telegram,** in which Germany hinted that Mexico should invade the United States, and a German professor at Cornell University set off a bomb in the U.S. Senate and shot J. P. Morgan. In heated reaction, America entered the war in April 1917.

America, now a true superpower, swung the tide, and the war ended in 1918. In all, ten million soldiers died in World War I, and another twenty million people died of disease and hunger. The war killed nearly an entire generation of young men. Many people believed that it had been the war to end all wars. But that idea would prove extremely naive.

★ ★ ★

AMERICA SPEAKS

"The way to make money is to buy when blood is running in the streets."

—John D. Rockefeller

"Upon the sacredness of property civilization itself depends . . . Not evil, but good, has come to the race from the accumulation of wealth by those who have had the ability and energy to produce it."

—Andrew Carnegie, from his article "Wealth" in the *North American Review*, 1890

"Year by year man's liberties are trampled underfoot at the bidding of corporations and trusts, rights are invaded and law perverted. In all ages wherever a tyrant has shown himself, he has always found some willing judge to clothe that tyranny in the robes of legality, and modern capitalism has proven no exception to the rule."

—Samuel Gompers (1894), leader of the American Federation of Labor from 1886 to 1924

★★★CHAPTER 11:★★★
Jazz Age

INTRO

As nations often do after wars, America fell into a policy of isolationism in the 1920s. The United States stayed out of European affairs and severely restricted immigration. Leaving the ideals of the **Progressive Era** behind, America in the twenties was back to its pro-business stance. And though they weren't drinking in public, thanks to Prohibition, Americans had lots of new entertainment to distract them: jazz music, new styles of dancing, radio broadcasts, and the first "talking" motion pictures.

Langston Hughes

LYRICS

Twenties came in like a lion;
by the end, that lion was dying,
couldn't even pounce.
Jazz Age, Dukes and Counts,
big-band swing time make you bounce.
You know what this is: **Prohibition**,
no liquor sipping,
no-oh, we're **bootlegging**.
Like **Al Capone,** running Chicago,
organized crime, making the dough,
moving more booze than Busch is,
ladies for the first time,
shaking their tushes.
Flappers happening,
fellows looking dapper,
old folks cheeks turning red
like the snapper.
Big business is back in business,
big business is good for US, idn't it?
Fundamentalist Tennessee
trying evolution,
the **Scopes Monkey**.
KKK wearing their sheets,
as if they weren't white enough,
those dumb junkies.
Black leader **Marcus Garvey**
packs it up,
thinks blacks should return to Africa.
My favorite poet loves the blues,
king of the **Harlem Renaissance**, it's
Langston Hughes . . .

CONTEXT AND BACKGROUND

Twenties came in like a lion; by the end, that lion was dying . . .
Starting in 1921, America experienced a decade of prosperity that fueled a growing consumer culture. Automobiles (invented twenty years earlier) finally became affordable for a large number of Americans, who also began purchasing new home appliances: refrigerators, vacuum cleaners, and washing machines.

But all this prosperity came crashing down on **Black Monday**, October 28, 1929. Soon the stock market had lost $30 billion, ushering in the **Great Depression**.

Jazz Age, Dukes and Counts, big-band swing time make you bounce . . .
Large numbers of African-Americans had come North during World War I to find manufacturing jobs. In the twenties, new African-American communities flourished in Chicago, New York, and elsewhere. Jazz music (which had been invented by African-Americans in the South around 1900) now found enormous popularity with white audiences as well.

The music moved from bluesy, New Orleans beginnings to orchestra-inspired big bands with twelve to twenty members. These big bands played danceable swing music in clubs and halls. King Oliver, Louis Armstrong, Billie Holiday, Duke Ellington, and Count Basie were some of the newly famous jazz musicians.

Prohibition, no liquor sipping, no-oh, we're bootlegging . . .
Most Americans (women in particular) thought immoral behavior and drinking were like hot days and snow cones: they went hand in hand.

Women couldn't yet vote, but they demonstrated their political influence when the United States outlawed the manufacturing and selling of alcohol in 1920 by passing the Eighteenth Amendment.

But those who lived during Prohibition found many ways to skirt the law. Bootleggers smuggled liquor from the West Indies and Canada, and new secret clubs called **speakeasies** appeared in major cities, replacing bars.

Like Al Capone, running Chicago, organized crime ...

In fact, the Prohibition didn't eradicate immoral behavior so much as it allowed a new class of organized thieves to flourish. Gangsters throughout America got enormously rich from distributing illegal alcohol. Al Capone, the famous mob boss of Chicago, built an empire of organized crime entirely based on controlling liquor.

Ladies for the first time, shaking their tushes ...

If you were to go to a club tonight, just know that all the wild gyrating, hip-swiveling, bumping and grinding, and freaking actually have their American roots in the Jazz Age. New styles of dancing, including the Charleston and the Black Bottom, became the hot dances for blacks *and* whites. White people had historically danced with their legs and their shoulders. To jazz music, they began dancing with their hips.

Flappers happening, fellows looking dapper ...

With the new music and dances came new social mores. While a huge portion of young Americans were still very conservative, a visible group seemed to embody the Jazz Age: drinking

illegal liquor, dancing with suggestive moves to hot music, and maybe even having premarital sex. A new fashion icon was the **flapper**, the young woman with tomboy hair, a frilly skirt, and an appetite for illegal booze. However, very few women of the time actually fit this description.

Big business is back in business, big business is good for US, idn't it ...

In 1920 **Warren G. Harding** promised a "return to normalcy" and won the presidential election by a landslide. What this really meant was a return to pro-business government policies. His successors, **Calvin Coolidge** and **Herbert Hoover**, continued these policies. Business boomed and the stock market grew. But speculative investments inflated the unregulated market, and disaster was looming.

Fundamentalist Tennessee trying evolution, the Scopes Monkey ...

Darwin's theory of evolution was scandalous. It seemed to say that thousands of years of religious teachings were mere fables. The question soon became: what do we teach students? The Tennessee legislature made its decision and outlawed teaching evolution in 1925. A man named Scopes was soon arrested for breaking this law, and some famous figures flocked to the trial.

Former presidential candidate **William Jennings Bryan** was there to defend Christianity, and a lawyer named **Clarence Darrow** (supported by the **American Civil Liberties Union**) was there to defend evolution. This legal showdown became known as the Scopes Monkey Trial. In the end, Scopes lost the case and had to pay $100. But the American public had listened as Darrow exposed the inconsistencies of Bryan's fundamentalist religious views.

KKK wearing their sheets . . .

Originally created just after the Civil War by racist Confederate soldiers and Southern churchmen, the Ku Klux Klan experienced a resurgence in the 1920s. This was partly due to D. W. Griffith's groundbreaking film **Birth of a Nation** (1915), which exploited racist stereotypes and glorified the Klan. The Klan also launched a successful membership drive and recruited American Protestants who wanted to prevent blacks, Catholics, and Jews from achieving any level of power in America. The Klan used violence and the threat of violence to secure its goals. After fading in the thirties, the KKK would again emerge after World War II.

Black leader Marcus Garvey packs it up, thinks blacks should return to Africa . . .

In increasingly large numbers, African-Americans began organizing and advocating for themselves. **W. E. B. Du Bois** led the National Association for the Advancement of Colored People (**NAACP**) and called for integration and equal treatment.

Other blacks figured "let's get out of here." Marcus Garvey urged blacks to return to Africa and establish an independent nation. Garvey was found guilty of fraud in 1923 and was deported to Jamaica.

King of the Harlem Renaissance, it's Langston Hughes . . .

African-American culture was flourishing in the jazz clubs of New Orleans, Chicago, and New York, but this wave of creative output wasn't limited to music. During the Harlem Renaissance, poets and authors brought the black experience to the printed page. Langston Hughes used blues forms and motifs in his politically charged poems, including his famous "The Weary Blues" in 1926. Later he became a communist and began advocating for major political change in America with such poems as "One More 'S' in the U. S. A."

★ ★ ★

AMERICA SPEAKS

"I am like any other man. All I do is supply a demand."

—Al Capone

"I have always felt that doubt was the beginning of wisdom, and the fear of God was the end of wisdom."

—Clarence Darrow, lawyer in the Scopes Monkey Trial

". . . They'll see how beautiful I am / And be ashamed— / I, too, am America."

—Langston Hughes, from the poem "I, too, am America"

CHAPTER 12

FDR (Interlude)

INTRO

Booming economies are often based on some level of speculation, which is really just another word for betting. For example, in the 1830s, "speculators" in the Midwest bet that if they bought land, the prices would eventually go up and they could make a profit. The problem comes when too many investments are based on speculations that don't come to fruition. This often results in a crash.

On October 28, 1929, the stock market crashed. Within weeks of "Black Monday," the stock market had lost $30 billion and the Great Depression was upon America and much of the world.

The Great Depression was the worst economic depression in history. In

Migrants

America, 30,000 businesses failed in 1932 alone. In 1933 the unemployment rate was at 25 percent. Migrant workers left their homes in search of opportunities that didn't exist. **Herbert Hoover**, president at the time, did very little other than assure America that "everything is going to be just fine . . . any day now." It wasn't.

In the 1932 election, Hoover was defeated by **Franklin Delano Roosevelt,** who would go on to be the longest-sitting president in U.S. history.

TEXT

"This is preeminently the time to speak the truth, the whole truth, frankly and boldly. Nor need we shrink from honestly facing conditions in our country today. This great nation will endure as it has endured, will revive and will prosper.

So first of all, let me assert my firm belief that the only thing we have to fear is fear itself: nameless, unreasoning, unjustified terror, which paralyzes needed efforts to convert retreat into advance."

—Franklin D. Roosevelt, from the first inaugural address, March 4, 1933

CONTEXT AND BACKGROUND

FDR went to work quickly. In his famous first hundred days, he launched a **New Deal** for national recovery. His attitude was basically, "Let's try a thousand things to fix the depression, and if most of them fail, who cares, at least we're doing something." With this mindset, Roosevelt and Congress passed so many acts that he didn't even have time to read them all (but he signed them). A conservative Supreme Court declared many of these acts unconstitutional, but Roosevelt and Congress kept passing them anyway.

Two years later, Roosevelt redoubled his efforts with the **Second New Deal**, the centerpiece of which was the **Works Progress Administration (WPA)** that eventually pumped $11 billion into the economy and helped pull the nation out of the terrible slump. He also created **Social Security**, which taxes people and then pays them a stipend when they retire.

Roosevelt was a chummy and charismatic leader. Under Hoover, 25,000 disgruntled and impoverished World War I veterans had marched to Washington to demand their war bonus. Seeing that these ragged men were disrupting the capital city, Hoover sent out the military—tanks and all—to squash the rebellion. When this "**Bonus Army**" returned under Roosevelt's administration, the president sent out his wife, **Eleanor**, to meet with them and serve them tea.

Roosevelt also invented "**fireside chats**," which were radio broadcasts that rallied popular support for his policies and gave hope to a hurting nation.

CHAPTER 13

Would You Drop It?

INTRO

It might sound trite, but just as with emotional depression, the best way to climb out of an economic depression is to trust that tomorrow will be better than today. When investors and workers believe that the future will bring something positive, they begin to put their money back into the system.

FDR helped get America out of the depression by giving them hope. His speeches and **fireside chats** made Americans believe that the country could turn itself around. In Europe, the leaders of some countries were instilling hope in their populaces by blaming foreigners for their countries' woes. A fascist dictator named Mussolini blamed communists and

Stalin, Roosevelt, and Churchill

foreigners for Italy's problems. In Germany, a fascist named Hitler placed the blame on Jews, foreigners, and those who opposed German power.

Soon another giant war began raging. America, however, stood back. It would take a direct attack on American soil before the United States joined World War II.

Would You Drop It?

LYRICS

Hitler's not the only **fascist,**
only the most famous,
Mussolini in Italy,
and **Franco's** Spanish.
Rose in the thirties, thanks to their
people's pain and anguish,
Depression era inflation
raising prices and panic.
Hitler makes Germans feel good by
puffin' them up,
like "It's not you, it's the **Jews**
that are messing us up."
So called "work-camps" for **Catholics,
Gypsies**, and Jews,
and any woman or man who dared
question his views.
America on another tip, **isolationist,**
don't want to get involved in one of
y'all big wars.
We're trying to recover
from our own depression,
FDR leading us, **New Deal,**
new direction.
German **U-boat**, submarines,
and you know what I mean,
sink British ships, Americans get uneasy.
While European is falling to Hitler,
Americans are like, "tweedle-dee . . ."

It's peaceful, hot Hawaiian sun rising in
the morning,

CONTEXT AND BACKGROUND

Hitler's not the only fascist, only the most famous . . .
What is a fascist? Fascism is generally a military dictatorship based on strong nationalist sentiment, racism, and the suppression of opposition by using force, such as Hitler's regime. Fascists come to power by exploiting patriotism, racism, and fear. Mussolini invented the term in 1925 and used it proudly.

Mussolini in Italy, and Franco's Spanish . . .
Benito Mussolini, also called *Il Duce* ("the leader"), installed himself as Italy's dictator in 1925. Mussolini blamed foreigners for Italy's problems and promised to get Italy's notoriously late trains running on time (he did not). He also built up Italy's military and, in 1935, invaded **Ethiopia**.
   The third famous fascist, **Francisco Franco,** overthrew the Spanish government in 1936 in the **Spanish Civil War**. Franco and his fascist rebels won the war largely because of military aid from Germany and Italy.

Rose in the thirties, thanks to their people's pain and anguish . . .
Adolph Hitler came to power largely by blaming outsiders for the humiliating position in which Germany found itself after the **Treaty of Versailles** ended World War I. War reparations, the hyperinflation of 1923, and then the international economic depression all fed the fascist rhetoric of blaming outsiders.

Hitler makes Germans feel good by puffin' them up, like "It's not you, it's the Jews that are messing us up" . . .
Hitler was a failed painter with a weird

mustache, but he was extremely skilled at giving rousing, patriotic speeches. His **National Socialist (Nazi) Party** took power in 1933. Hitler blamed the economic and social problems of Germany on foreigners and Jews (who, he argued, controlled the world's finances). Europe had a long history of anti-Semitism, and Germans (and others) found it easy to blame Jews for their problems.

So called "work-camps" for Catholics, Gypsies, and Jews . . .

The original concentration camps were built in Germany in 1933 as a place to keep

Adolph Hitler

"undesirables." Jews, Catholics, Gypsies, communists, gay people, the mentally and physically disabled, Polish intellectuals, and others were shipped to these prison camps to work in slave labor.

Actual extermination camps weren't built until 1941. These death camps would contribute to the murder of at least six million Jews and four million gentiles (mostly Polish gentiles and gypsies) during the Holocaust.

America on another tip, isolationist . . .

America in the twenties and thirties was isolationist, totally uninterested in another European war that seemed looming. As European nations were arming, America passed a series of **Neutrality Acts** (1935–37) that prohibited arms sales to warring nations. These acts were supported by prominent American anti-Semites such as **Charles Lindbergh** and **Henry Ford,** who didn't want America selling arms to Britain and France.

We're trying to recover from our own depression, FDR leading us, New Deal . . .

Roosevelt was attuned to the country's antiwar sentiment, but after Hitler invaded Czechoslovakia, it became clearer that fascist powers in Europe would soon face off against Britain and France. In the summer of 1939, Roosevelt urged Congress to revise the Neutrality Acts to allow for arms sales to warring nations if they paid in cash. This **cash-and-carry policy** aided the **Allies**, without committing the United States to war.

German U-boat, submarines . . . sink British ships, Americans get uneasy . . .

America continued to stay out of the war as Hitler invaded Poland, Denmark, Norway, Belgium, the Netherlands, and France. Hitler

America's navy stretching and yawning.
Low on the horizon, hundreds of planes
are rising.
Someone sees something,
"eh, that's probably nothing."
But those are **Japanese** fighters and
bombers, dropping some bombs upon
us, harm us with preemptive strikes,
breaking the dam and the dyke.
It's a date people remember like 9-11,
Pearl Harbor, 1941, December 7.

Would you drop-drop it?
Would you drop-drop it?
Would you drop-drop it?
Drop the bomb?
Would you drop the bomb?

Fast forward—rushed the beaches,
D-day's done,
liberated **France** and **Italy**,
blazing guns.
Germany surrenders,
Hitler commits suicide,
he couldn't stand to die
in front of the world's eyes.
Southeast Asia, war's still raging,
we're **island hopping** like hopscotch,
boys with bloody faces.
Spring 1945, FDR dies. In steps
Truman, big man, but only human.
Here's the situation:
you're about to invade **Japan.**

rode into Paris in his Mercedes with his one arm
extended, happy as a clam on June 23, 1940. The
Nazis then began bombing British cities during
the summer-long **Battle of Britain.**

In 1941, with the **Axis powers** now in
control of most of Europe, German submarines
(U-boats) torpedoed two American destroyers,
killing more than a hundred Americans. America
was then on the brink of joining the war.

**Low on the horizon, hundreds of planes
are rising. Someone sees something, "eh,
that's probably nothing" . . .**
The United States had a naval base at Pearl
Harbor in Hawaii. It was early in the morning
on December 7 when two U.S. Army privates
saw something strange on their radar screen:
dozens of planes appearing out of the
Northeast. The men were alarmed and
reported the sighting, but they were told that it
was probably just a delivery of new B-17 planes;
nothing to worry about.

**But those are Japanese fighters and
bombers, dropping some bombs
upon us . . .**
What they actually saw was the first wave of
183 Japanese fighter planes. It was a surprise
attack on America, and it was amazingly effective:
19 ships were sunk, 292 aircraft destroyed, and
2,403 Americans killed.

Breaking the dam and the dyke . . .
This was the event needed to catalyze America
into joining the war, the straw that broke the
camel's back. On December 8, the day after the
strike, Congress declared war on Japan. On
December 11, Germany and Italy joined Japan
and declared war on the United States. The
United States was now fighting a war in Europe
and a war in the Pacific.

Fast forward—rushed the beaches, D-day's done . . .

The Allies chose to concentrate on Europe before attacking Japan. With **Operation Torch**, U.S. troops under **General Dwight D. Eisenhower** invaded North Africa, forcing a **Vichy** (German-controlled) France surrender in 1942. In 1943 Allied troops invaded Italy and began pushing the Nazi lines back toward Germany.

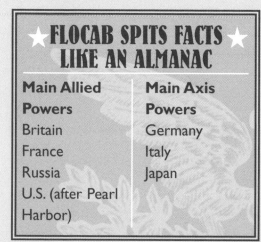

★ FLOCAB SPITS FACTS LIKE AN ALMANAC ★

Main Allied Powers	Main Axis Powers
Britain	Germany
France	Italy
Russia	Japan
U.S. (after Pearl Harbor)	

On June 6, 1944, D-Day, the Allies launched the largest sea-to-land invasion force in history. In the middle of the night, thousands of boats landed on French beaches and pushed the Germans back into France after days of bloody battles. It would be more than a year before Germany surrendered, though German ranks were then growing thin thanks to Russian forces attacking from the east.

Germany surrenders, Hitler commits suicide . . .

On April 30, 1945, while Russian bombs fell on Berlin, Hitler descended into a bunker with his mistress, **Eva Braun**, to get married. He then poisoned her and killed himself. Germany surrendered a week later.

Southeast Asia, war's still raging, we're island hopping like hopscotch . . .

In the **Pacific Theater** of World War II, the Japanese had conquered hundreds of small islands from New Guinea up to parts of mainland China. They controlled 10 percent of

U.S. soldier deaths might number a
million.
The Japanese fight with code of the
Samurai,
fight to the death, it's honorable to die.
Secret new weapon you've got and
you're not telling,
split atoms like a sledge hammer splits
watermelons.
Test it in July, **desert of New Mexico**,
it blows and you know mushroom
clouds fill the sky.
The **Russians** might declare war, and if
they do,
the Japanese might have no choice, but
to lay down their troops.
That's a chance. You've got the bombs.
You've got the planes.
This is war: the moral dilemma drives
you insane.
120,000 civilian lives on the line.
Clocks ticking, *tic-tock*, you're running out
of time.
What would Jesus do?
What would Buddha do?
What would Abraham do?
What would Muhammad do?
What would you do?

Would you drop-drop it?
Would you drop-drop it?
Would you drop-drop it?
Drop the bomb?
Would you drop the bomb?

the Earth's surface. The U.S. Navy attacked the
Japanese, island-hopping toward Japan from the
Central Pacific, while the Army moved from
island to island in the south.

Spring 1945, FDR dies. In steps Truman . . .
The Constitution didn't limit the number of
terms a president could hold office. By
stepping aside after two terms, George
Washington had set a precedent that every
other president followed. That is, until FDR.
FDR was elected to a fourth term in 1944, but
he died of a cerebral hemorrhage the
following April, just weeks before Hitler killed
himself. **Harry S. Truman** was sworn in as
president on April 12. In 1951 the states
ratified the **Twenty-Second Amendment**
to the Constitution, which limits the president
to two elected terms.

**Here's the situation: you're about to
invade Japan . . .**
Truman inherited some major decisions.
Though the war in Europe was nearly finished,
the war with Japan wasn't over yet. The United
States had pushed the Japanese out of the
Philippines, but an attack on Japan itself was
still looming.

**U.S. soldier deaths might number a
million . . .**
U.S. generals told Truman that an assault on
Japan could cost the United States between half
a million and a million casualties. **General
MacArthur** estimated that the Japanese would
continue guerilla-style resistance for ten years.
Some reports indicated that the Japanese were
arming civilians with sharpened bamboo spears,
in addition to their six million devoted troops.
Though losing the war, the Japanese resolutely
refused to surrender.

The Japanese fight with code of the Samurai ...

The Japanese had continually surprised Americans with a fighting style they inherited from the Samurai tradition: soldiers and civilians alike would rather die than be taken hostage. They had also launched 2,800 **kamikaze** attacks, in which small planes stuffed with bombs tried to smash into ships.

Secret new weapon you've got and you're not telling, split atoms ...

In 1939 **Albert Einstein** had written a letter to Roosevelt stating his hypothesis that a new type of bomb could be built based on a nuclear chain reaction. Roosevelt created the **Manhattan Project** to build this atomic bomb. Two days after Truman became president, he was told the top-secret information: the United States was developing an atomic bomb that had the destructive power of 20,000 tons of TNT. A test in July in the New Mexico desert was successful.

The Russians might declare war ...

Having defeated the Germans in Eastern Europe, **Joseph Stalin** was now eyeing Japan, trying to decide whether to declare war. Some accounts state that Truman already knew that Russia was going to enter the war and that dropping the atomic bombs was unnecessary. Others argue that Truman didn't know about Russia's intentions. Others believe that Truman dropped the bombs to show off U.S. power to the Russians, who were already emerging as rivals on the world stage.

This is war: the moral dilemma drives you insane . . .

When is killing justified? At times of war? When are wars justified? When is it okay to kill someone?

120,000 civilian lives on the line . . .

Truman did drop the bomb. In fact, he ordered two bombs to be dropped. On August 6, 1945, an American plane dropped the first bomb over **Hiroshima**, killing more than 70,000 people and injuring just as many. Three days later, America dropped another atomic bomb on **Nagasaki**, killing 40,000 and injuring 60,000 people. The same day, Stalin declared war on Japan and invaded Manchuria. The Japanese surrendered on August 11. We know Truman dropped the bomb. What would you do?

★ ★ ★

AMERICA SPEAKS

"We have discovered the most terrible bomb in the history of the world. It may be the fire destruction prophesied in the Euphrates valley Ersa, after Noah and his fabulous Ark. Anyway we 'think' we have found a way to cause the disintegration of the atom . . .

This weapon is to be used against Japan between now and August 10th. I have told the Sec. of War, Mr. Stimson, to use it so that military objectives and soldiers and sailors are the target and not women and children. Even if the Japs are savages, ruthless, merciless and fanatic, we as the leaders of the world for the common welfare cannot drop this terrible bomb on the old Capital or the new . . . The target will be a purely military one . . . It is certainly a good thing for the world that Hitler's crowd or Stalin's did not discover this atomic bomb. It seems to be the most terrible thing ever discovered, but it can be made to be the most useful."

—Harry Truman, from his diaries

CHAPTER 14

Let Freedom Ring

Slavery ended in America with the Civil War. But racist local governments (and a generally racist American population) worked hard during Reconstruction to prevent blacks from achieving real freedom, let alone any kind of equality.

In 1896 the Supreme Court decision in **Plessy v. Ferguson** made "separate but equal" the law of the land, and soon the South passed hundreds of local **Jim Crow** laws to keep blacks out of white restaurants, factories, train cars, and schools. Jim Crow laws also kept blacks away from the ballot through ballot taxes, literacy requirements, and violent intimidation. Lynching, usually on the pretext that a black man had raped a white woman (one of the biggest Southern fears) occurred throughout the South. As **Billie Holiday** would sing in her 1940's hit "**Strange Fruit**," "black bodies swinging in the Southern breeze, strange fruit hanging from the poplar trees."

For African-Americans, freedom was a dream deferred. It took a large number of people willing to fight for their rights to change the racist status quo in America.

Martin Luther King Jr.

92

Let Freedom Ring

LYRICS

*So even though we face the difficulties
of today and tomorrow,
I still have a dream.
It is a dream deeply rooted
in the American dream.
I have a dream that one day this nation
will rise up and live out
the true meaning of its creed:
We hold these truths to be self-evident
that all men are created equal.
I have a dream . . .*

It would take a nation of millions to
hold us back.
Brown v. Board opened some doors.
Back then they called all blacks
Negroes,
we kick it off the top sort of like
cerebrals.
Separate isn't equal, when in practice.
My school's a shack. *Mine is a palace!*
Do I have to sit in the back of the bus?
That's wackness.
Second-class citizen on account of
my blackness.
They say to change the world,
you've got to take a stand.
Rosa Parks took a seat,
changed the face of the land.
Martin had a plan that even if you want
to change the world

CONTEXT AND BACKGROUND

Brown v. Board opened some doors . . .
The first big victory for Civil Rights came in
1954 when the Supreme Court decided that
"separate but equal" in schools was
unconstitutional. The case was
Brown v. Board of Education of Topeka.
Chief Justice Earl Warren wrote in the
unanimous decision that "separate educational
facilities are inherently unequal" because the
system "generates a feeling of inferiority . . . that
may affect [the minority students'] hearts and
minds in a way unlikely ever to be undone."

In overturning Plessy v. Ferguson, the court
had made a bold statement against racial
discrimination. Most Southern states balked at
the decision and changed nothing. Resistance
was so aggressive in Little Rock, Arkansas, that
Eisenhower sent federal troops to force the
schools to desegregate in 1957.

Separate isn't equal, when in practice . . .
In *Brown v. Board of Education*, the Supreme
Court ruled that even when the schools were
physically identical, separation causes inequality.
But the schools for whites and the schools for
blacks (or "coloreds" as they were called) were
very rarely identical. White schools often
received ten times the funding that black
schools received.

**Rosa Parks took a seat, changed the face
of the land . . .**
The *Brown v. Board of Education* decision didn't
end segregation in the South. It just ended
segregation in schools. Blacks still had to drink
from separate water fountains, go to different
movie theaters, go to different restaurants, and

sit in the back of buses and give up their seats when white people got on.

On a December day in 1955, a forty-three-year-old seamstress named Rosa Parks boarded a bus after a long day at work in **Montgomery, Alabama**. Parks looked for a seat in the "colored" section at the back of the bus. Not finding one, she took a seat in the middle. When a group of white people got on the bus, the operator yelled out "niggers move back," but Parks didn't move.

Parks was quickly arrested and within hours the African-American community in Montgomery was uniting. They were led by the young minister at Rosa Parks's church, twenty-seven-year-old **Martin Luther King Jr.** King organized a powerful and effective **bus boycott** in Montgomery. In 1956 the Supreme Court upheld a lower court's decision outlawing segregation on buses.

Inspired by the people like Thoreau and Gandhi . . .

King believed that the best way to bring about equality was through nonviolent civil disobedience. King was inspired by **Henry David Thoreau**, who had written about the moral obligation to break immoral laws and had refused to pay taxes for the Mexican-American War. King was also inspired by **Mahatma Gandhi**, who had led India in a tremendously successful, nonviolent overthrow of British colonial rule.

King was a religious man who believed deeply in the Christian teachings of hope, forgiveness, love, and acceptance. These ideals directly influenced his strategies for achieving civil rights.

A pacifist in the war without an army . . .

Martin Luther King might not have had an army, but he did have followers. In 1957 he went to

Atlanta to form the **Southern Christian Leadership Conference (SCLC)**, which organized sit-ins at businesses that discriminated against blacks.

MLK had a dream, took it mainstream . . .

By advocating nonviolence and tolerance, King was able to sell his message to blacks and whites alike. Unlike more radical civil rights leaders like Malcolm X, King met with presidents Eisenhower, Kennedy, and Johnson to discuss policy. Before the **March on Washington** in 1963, when King delivered his famous "I have a dream" speech, President Kennedy spoke with King and told him to make sure the tone of the march wasn't too violent, otherwise Congress might not pass the Civil Rights Act.

Civil Rights Bill, Voting Rights Act, they passed . . .

The powerful March on Washington drew 250,000 civil rights supporters to the Capitol's steps, but Republicans in Congress still refused to pass a civil rights bill. After Kennedy's assassination, Johnson became president and outlined a **Great Society** program for America, part of which was to achieve racial equality. Johnson pushed the **Civil Rights Act**, which outlawed racial discrimination in public facilities, through Congress in 1964. This was the same year that Dr. King was awarded the **Nobel Peace Prize**. A year later Congress passed the **Voting Rights Act**, which encouraged black enfranchisement and protected black voters. It was a major victory for civil rights.

Malcolm picked up X and dropped his slave name . . .

Not everyone was happy with King's *Soul Power* movement, though. Some African-Americans felt that King's nonviolent, turn-the-continued

that don't mean you've got to kill
another man.
Inspired by the people like **Thoreau**
and **Gandhi,**
a **pacifist** in the war without an army.
'Cause they can't harm me,
no matter how the end seems.
I wonder if Mr. King
is still having dreams . . .

Let freedom ring . . .
I have a dream . . .
This must become true. . .
So let freedom ring . . .

MLK had a dream, took it mainstream.
Civil Rights Bill, Voting Rights Act,
they passed.
A modern-day Jesus,
turning the other cheek,
some blacks like "dawg, that's weak.
I'm not looking to get beat
deep into next week,
my everyday life is police brutality."
Malcolm picked up X
and dropped his slave name,
radical change, "defense by any means."
Went on hajj to **Mecca**,
said "let God protect ya.
Whites and blacks, yeah,
we're in this together."
But there are **race riots,**
people are dying,

other-cheek mentality was too weak to
effectively deal with racial discrimination and
violence. One of the first leaders of this **Black
Power** movement was Malcolm X.

Born Malcolm Little in Omaha, Nebraska,
Malcolm escaped a fire set to his house by white
men when he was four. Later in Boston, he was
arrested for burglary. While in jail he decided to
drop his "slave name" and adopted "X" instead,
arguing that his true, African last name had been
lost on the slave ships.

He soon became the most prominent
minister for the **Nation of Islam**, a religious
and political institution under the leadership of
Elijah Muhammad.

Radical change, "defense by any means" . . .
Malcolm X believed that blacks could only
achieve equality and freedom through radical
change. He called Martin Luther King's March on
Washington a "Farce on Washington."

He also famously said, "We declare our right
on this earth. . . to be a human being, to be
respected as a human being, to be given the
rights of a human being in this society, on this
earth, in this day, which we intend to bring into
existence *by any means necessary*."

**Went on hajj to Mecca, said "let God
protect ya. Whites and blacks, yeah, we're
in this together" . . .**
In 1964 Malcolm broke with the Nation of
Islam. A few months later he took a pilgrimage
to the holy city of Mecca, a religious journey
known as the *hajj*. In Mecca he experienced a
kind of spiritual rebirth that caused him to
reconsider many of his views toward white
people. He came back to the United States
with a much softer message, still advocating for
civil rights, but offering a more conciliatory
view toward whites.

Unfortunately, Malcolm X, JFK, and MLK weren't the only prominent Americans to be assassinated during the 1960s.

- **Medgar Evers,** an African-American civil rights activist from Mississippi was assassinated by a white racist in 1963.
- **Robert Kennedy** was one of John F. Kennedy's two younger brothers (Massachusetts senator Ted Kennedy is the other). He served as the attorney general during his brother's administration and used his position to fight corruption, racism, and organized crime. After JFK's assassination, Robert became a senator from New York and began voicing his opposition to the Vietnam War. He decided to run for president in 1968, and many Democrats were ecstatic about electing him. But just after the California primary, and just two months after the death of King, Robert Kennedy was shot and killed. The killer, Sirhan B. Sirhan, claimed he had killed him because Kennedy had supported Israel's Six-Day War.

But there are race riots, people are dying, warfare in Watts . . .

Meanwhile blood was being spilled all over the country. In 1963 a Birmingham church was bombed, killing three African-American girls. Three civil rights advocates were murdered in Mississippi in 1964 (*Mississippi Burning*). In 1965 Malcolm X was assassinated.

It was in the summer of 1965 when a white police officer pulled over a young black driver to check him for drunk driving. This was in **Watts**, an all-black, run-down neighborhood in Los Angeles. The officer arrested the young man, but a crowd had gathered. By the time the officer called for backup, the crowd had grown larger and angrier. They began hurtling rocks and bottles at the officers. The next day, the hot Los Angeles sun brought no respite: the protest had grown into a full-scale riot with thousands of angry African-Americans marching through the streets with guns and Molotov cocktails. They set Watts on fire.

Thousands of national guardsmen were called in, and a battle raged for six days. The riot killed thirty-four people, injured more than 1,000, and caused $50 to $100 million in damage. The following hot summers brought more race riots, most notably in Detroit, Michigan, and Newark, New Jersey.

So JFK? He got assassinated . . .

The sixties were an amazingly turbulent time in America. While civil rights battles were being fought in legislatures and on the streets, a series of presidents, fearful of Soviet domination, brought the nation further and further into a war in Vietnam, a small country on the other side of the world. America was then rocked by the assassinations of many important figures (and heroes to many) within the course of just a few years.

John F. Kennedy was assassinated on November 22, 1963. He had gone to Texas to drum up support for his reelection campaign and was traveling in a parade route through Dallas when he was shot by **Lee Harvey Oswald** from the sixth story of a nearby building. A tremendous amount of controversy surrounds Kennedy's assassination, with conspiracy theorists arguing that the

warfare in **Watts**, tear gas,
bullets are flying.
So **JFK?**
He got assassinated.
MLK?
He got assassinated.
Malcolm X?
He got assassinated.
So it's up to us
to keep that dream alive . . .

Let freedom ring . . .
I have a dream . . .
This must become true
So let freedom ring . . .

Let us not seek to satisfy
our thirst for freedom,
by drinking from the cup
of bitterness and hatred.

government's official story (that Oswald acted alone) doesn't make sense. Oswald himself couldn't be questioned because he was shot and killed two days later by an angry nightclub owner, Jack Ruby.

The charismatic president who had captured America's heart was dead.

MLK? He got assassinated . . .
On April 4, 1968, Martin Luther King was assassinated. He was shot and killed while speaking on a balcony at a motel in Memphis, Tennessee. He was killed by James Earl Ray, a white racist.

The country fell into chaos. In more than one hundred cities, blacks took to the streets in anger. The riots led to forty-six deaths and 27,000 arrests. The immediate and lasting effects of the death of Martin Luther King on America are impossible to quantify.

Malcolm X? He got assassinated . . .
Malcolm X was shot and killed in the Audubon Ballroom in Harlem on February 21, 1965. Unlike JFK and MLK, Malcolm was living in a state of panic. Two weeks earlier, his house had been firebombed. The men arrested for his death were three members of the Nation of Islam, though the truth behind the assassination (as with many others) remains mysterious.

★ ★ ★

AMERICA SPEAKS

"I refuse to accept the view that mankind is so tragically bound to the starless midnight of racism and war that the bright daybreak of peace and brotherhood can never become reality. I believe that unarmed truth and unconditional love will have the final word."

—Martin Luther King Jr., accepting the Nobel Peace Prize (1964)

★★★ CHAPTER 15: ★★★
Guide to the Songs

Who Discovered It?

Back before buffalo wings at Domino's . . .
Dominos is a fast-food restaurant chain serving pizza, chicken wings, and other food items.

Buffalo roamed . . . the range, home of the free, land of the brave . . .
These lines combine phrases from the "The Star-Spangled Banner" and "Home on the Range," the state song of Kansas.

Hut to hut like quarterbacks . . .
The quarterback in a game of football receives the ball from the snapper by shouting "hut, hut, hike" or another combination of prearranged words.

Putting holes in enemies' domes like the ozone . . .
Dome is a slang word for someone's head.

   The ozone layer is located in the upper part of the Earth's atmosphere and helps protect the planet from ultraviolet radiation. In the past sixty years, the amount of ozone in the atmosphere has noticeably decreased. There is now a large "ozone hole" over Antarctica.

I Want America

Sipping Henny. JK LOL BRB TTYL! :-)
Hennessey (or *Henny*) is a cognac that makes occasional appearances in rap videos. *JK* is instant messenger speak for "just kidding." *LOL* means "laughing out loud." *BRB* means "be right back." *TTYL* means "talk to you later."

Supplies shorter than Dora the Explorer . . .
Dora the Explorer is an animated character in a TV show of the same name aimed at preschoolers. While Dora's exact height is a mystery, a guesstimate would be that she is three feet tall.

98

Saw land calling "Hoo-Ah!" like Scent of a Woman ...
Scent of a Woman is a 1992 film starring Chris O'Donnell and Al Pacino. Pacino plays Lieutenant Colonel Frank Slade, a blind ex-marine who likes yelling, "hoo-ah!" "Hoo-ah" is a common affirmative yelled by soldiers in the U.S. military.

This Ain't Working

Like rubberneckers ...
Rubbernecker is a slang term for someone who cranes his or her neck to see something while passing by. Typically this term is used for motorists passing an accident who slow their cars to get a better look.

"Let's Twist Again," uh-huh, like Chubby Checker ...
Chubby Checker's single "Let's Twist Again" was the first record to go platinum. The idea here is that the Boston Tea Party actually *was* a party. With large crowds gathered to watch and applaud, it was much more of a Chubby Checker– style gathering than a covert military operation.

Hands be twitching more than Muhammad Ali's ...
Muhammad Ali is probably the greatest heavyweight boxer of all time. After an amazing life in the ring, he developed Pugilistic Parkinson's disease (aka Boxer's Syndrome), which restricts his speech and causes his hands to shake. He was awarded the Presidential Medal of Freedom in 2005.

Putting medal on them like they're honored ...
A typical, official way of honoring someone is by giving him or her a medal. (See Muhammad Ali above.) Musket bullets were not shaped like today's bullets; they were round, lead balls.

Guide to the Songs, Continued

Ducking out of trees like some Vietnamese . . .

The Vietcong (North Vietnamese sympathizers operating in South Vietnam) later perfected the very basic guerilla-fighting style used by the Minutemen. During the Vietnam War, the Vietcong avoided large-scale encounters with American troops. They developed hit-and-run and sniper tactics instead. After the initial skirmishes at Lexington and Concord, the American forces rarely used guerilla tactics in the Revolutionary War.

It's the U.S. (Bust the A)

Time for states to form up like Megatron . . .

Megatron is the robotic leader of the Decepticons from the TV show and comic book, *Transformers*. Megatron could transform from a gun into a humanoid robot.

It didn't have power like Masons . . .

Masons are members of the fraternal organization of Freemasons. Formed in Europe in 1717, this semisecret society took hold in America and became popular among the American elite. Many of the Founding Fathers were Masons, including John Hancock, Paul Revere, Benjamin Franklin, and George Washington. Washington, the first of fourteen U.S. presidents who were Masons, even wore a Masonic apron when he laid the cornerstone of the U.S. Capitol building.

In 1831 some citizens formed the Anti-Masonic Party to protest the perceived Masonic control of the government and the fact that an ex-Mason who wanted to publish Masonic secrets had recently been abducted and disappeared. The Anti-Masonic candidate for president received a respectable seven electoral votes in 1832, marking the first fairly successful third party in American politics.

It was too weak, like brittle bones on bubble boys . . .

The *bubble-boy* phenomenon comes from the stories of two boys in the seventies who really did live in bubbles within sterile hospital rooms: David Vetter and Ted DeVita, both of whom suffered from immune deficiencies. Since then, the bubble boy has become a kind of American trope featured in a Seinfeld episode, a Paul Simon lyric, and a recent movie staring Jake Gyllenhaal.

Break your government up like a Kit-Kat Bar . . .
A Kit-Kat Bar is a candy bar of chocolate-coated wafers. It comes in four individual pieces that you can break off. The current jingle used to promote the candy bar in America goes, "Gimme a break, gimme a break, break me off a piece of that Kit-Kat Bar."

Picks judges like Sam Alito . . .
In 2005 George W. Bush nominated Samuel Alito to the Supreme Court after Sandra Day O'Connor retired. Earlier that year, Bush nominated John Roberts who replaced the late Chief Justice William H. Rehnquist. Both nominees were approved by the Senate.

Bill of Rights

Sorry Alex, there's no *Double Jeopardy* . . .
Alex Trebek is the host of the popular television game show *Jeopardy!*. Once contestants pass the first round, they move on to *Double Jeopardy*, in which point values are doubled.

O.D.W.M.

Some lines from this track are based on lines from Outkast's "Skew It on the Bar-B" and Young MC's "Bust a Move."

He wanted people to choose their religion like dim sum . . .
Dim sum is a type of light Chinese meal consisting of a variety of choices that are typically wheeled around on a cart for customers to choose from.

Thought the Pres was too powerful like King Kong . . .
King Kong is a big gorilla with a big heart and the star of numerous movies, including *King Kong* (1933) and *King Kong* (2005).

Buy Louisiana with bonds. We're rich like Häagen Dazs . . .
Häagen Dazs makes creamy, rich ice cream. The company is from New York, but it took the name *Häagen Dazs* to make its ice cream sound exotic.

Guide to the Songs, Continued

We're the Hekawi like F-troop . . .

F-troop was a television comedy show from the 1960s. The Indian tribe in the show often got lost and would say, "Where the heck are we?" The original name of the tribe, the Fugawi, was changed after sponsors complained.

Guides them through Rockies like MapQuest . . .

MapQuest is a free online mapping software that outlines travel paths for trips.

Hamilton missed the mark like Crystal Pepsi . . .

In 1992 Pepsi unveiled Crystal Pepsi, the first mainstream clear cola. It was a total commercial failure. In 1993 *Saturday Night Live* parodied Crystal Pepsi with a fake advertisement for Crystal Gravy. The voiceover said, "Finally you can see your meat."

Levez les mains . . .

French for "raise your hands."

Free OJ, like Johnny Cochran . . .

Johnny Cochran was one of O. J. Simpson's "Dream Team" defense lawyers in the famous murder trial. Cochran actually used rhymes to help convince the jury that O. J. was innocent: "if it [the glove] doesn't fit, you must acquit." O. J. Simpson was found not guilty.

Men getting richer than Enron . . .

Enron Corporation is an enormous energy company based in Houston, Texas. In 2001, company officers used accounting fraud to make an enormous personal profit at the expense of shareholders.

Like Adolf Hitler, he had a Final Solution . . .

The "Final Solution of the Jewish Question" is a phrase coined by Adolf Eichmann, a top Nazi official under Hitler. The phrase refers to the German Nazis' plan to systematically kill the Jewish population of Europe during World War II.

Ghosts of the Civil War

The Senator from South Cakalak ...
Cakalak is a slang word for "Carolina." Calhoun was from South Carolina.

States' rights best thing since grits 'n' gravy ...
Grits are a traditional Southern breakfast food made from cornmeal. Grits are often eaten with butter, sugar, or gravy.

Like Dead Prez, boy, I'm an African ...
Dead Prez is a politically conscious hip-hop group. Its 2000 album, *Let's Get Free*, features "I'm a African," a song that connects American blacks to their African roots.

I wanted to be soft on the Confederacy like Huggies ...
Huggies are a brand of disposable diaper for babies.

Big Ballin' (in the Gilded Age)

I'm bigger than *Big Pimpin'*, I'm bigger than Jay-Z. He named his record company after me ...
Jay-Z (Shawn Carter) is a popular rapper from New York. He collaborated with Houston rappers Bun B and Pimp C on 2000's *Big Pimpin'*. He founded Roc-A-Fella Records in 1996. In 1999 Jay-Z launched Rocawear, a hip-hop clothing label.

I'm the O.G. ...
O.G. is street slang for "original gangster." The term initially referred to the founder of a street gang but now commonly refers to any older gang member. It also stands for "Oil and Gas."

With more oil than *Valdez* ...
The *Exxon Valdez* is the name of an oil tanker that, in 1989, hit a reef off of Prince William Sound and spilled eleven million gallons of crude oil into the ocean. Exxon (now ExxonMobil) is a descendant of John D. Rockefeller's Standard Oil Trust.

Guide to the Songs, Continued

Gobble up these Colonel Sanders like they're chicken feed ...
Colonel Sanders founded Kentucky Fried Chicken in 1952. Sanders (who was not actually a military colonel) invented the original recipe. After he sold his business, he became Kentucky Fried Chicken's spokesman, but he didn't hesitate to speak up against the company when he thought that quality was waning. In 1975 Kentucky Fried Chicken sued Harlan Sanders for calling the gravy "sludge" and "wallpaper paste."

The rest can't touch 'cause I'm higher than Marley ...
Bob Marley was a popular reggae musician from Jamaica. Marley often appears on dorm-room posters, smoking marijuana.

Jazz Age

Moving more booze than Busch is ...
Anheuser-Busch is the world's third-largest brewing company. It is based in St. Louis, Missouri. It produces Budweiser, Michelob, and Bacardi.

Old folks cheeks turning red like the snapper ...
Red snapper is a reef fish found off America's coast in the Atlantic Ocean. It is healthy and delicious.

Would You Drop It?

We're island hopping like hopscotch ...
Hopscotch is a game played on sidewalks, streets, and playgrounds throughout the world in different forms. The game involves throwing a stone or marker and then hopping on different squares. The game was originally developed in England as endurance training for British soldiers, who played hopscotch in full body armor.

Let Freedom Ring

It would take a nation of millions to hold us back . . .
The popular and political rap group Public Enemy released one of the most important hip-hop albums in 1988: **It Takes a Nation of Millions to Hold Us Back**. The album pitted Chuck D's lyrics (which explored institutional racism, police brutality, and American greed) over sample-heavy beats.

We kick it off the top sort of like cerebrals . . .
To "kick it off of the top (of the dome)" means to freestyle: make up rap lyrics in real time off the top of your head.

The word *cerebral* means "of, or relating to, the brain." Cerebrals are members of an obscure group with high IQs ("The Cerebral Society"), like the much more famous Mensa.

A modern-day Jesus, turning the other cheek . . .
"I say to you, do not resist one who is evil. But if any one strikes you on the right cheek, turn to him the other also; and if any one would sue you and take your coat, let him have your cloak as well . . . I say to you, love your enemies and pray for those who persecute you . . ." (from Matthew 5:38–45).

Appendices

Appendix 1

Guide to the Age of Exploration

Name	Sailing for	Areas Explored
Christopher Columbus	Spain	1492: Bahamas, Cuba, Haiti
		1493: Santo Domingo
John Cabot	England	1497–8: Nova Scotia, Newfoundland
Amerigo Vespucci	Spain	1499: Coast of South America
	Portugal	1501: Coast of South America
Ponce de León	Spain	1513–21: Florida
Ferdinand Magellan	Spain	1519: First person to sail around the globe
Hernando Cortés	Spain	1519–22: Conquered the Aztecs in Mexico
Francisco Pizarro	Spain	1530–36: Conquered the Incas in Peru
Hernando de Soto	Spain	1539–42: Southern U.S. coast
Jacques Cartier	France	1542: St. Lawrence River to Montreal
Samuel de Champlain	France	1608–25: Great Lakes; founded Quebec
Henry Hudson	Netherlands	1609–11: Hudson River

Appendix II

Guide to the Enlightenment

In medieval times, in Europe, the final word in almost every situation was the Christian Bible. Since peasants couldn't read the Bible (it was in Latin), the word of God was passed to them from powerful figures: priests, kings, and lords. These rulers weren't elected. They also exploited peasants for enormous economic gain and then sent them off to fight and die in wars, all in the name of God. Most people just followed the rules and didn't ask questions. There was no democracy. The people had little voice.

Then came the Age of Enlightenment. Some people start asking some *big* questions: *Why am I here? How do I know that I'm here? Why do I do the things I do?* Most of these thinkers believed in God, but they began to say, "Show me the logic":

—Descartes said: "I think therefore I am."

—Montaigne wore a necklace that said: "What do I know?"

—Spinoza said: "God doesn't have a personality. The natural world is God."

Some thinkers began to question governments themselves:

—Locke said: "A government is only legitimate if the people say it is."

—Rousseau said: "There is a social contract between the people and the government."

Locke believed firmly that governments do not *grant* rights. Men are born with rights (most Enlightenment thinkers still viewed women as second-class). Enlightenment thinkers came up with the stunning idea that governments should serve the people. If the government does not serve and represent the people, the people should rebel. If these ideas seem simple and obvious today, it just goes to show how important and influential the Enlightenment was in changing the way we see the world.

Appendices, Continued

Appendix III

Biblical References to Slavery

Old Testament

"When a slave owner strikes a male or female slave with a rod and the slave dies immediately, the owner shall be punished. But if the slave survives a day or two, there is no punishment; for the slave is the owner's property." (Exodus 21:20–21)

New Testament

"A disciple is not above the teacher, nor a slave above the master." (Matthew 10:24)

"Who then is the faithful and wise slave, whom his master has put in charge of his household, to give the other slaves their allowance of food at the proper time? Blessed is that slave whom his master will find at work when he arrives." (Matthew 24:45–46)

New Testament (the writings of Paul)

"Let all who are under the yoke of slavery regard their masters as worthy of all honor, so that the name of God and the teaching may not be blasphemed." (1 Timothy 6:1)

"Slaves, obey your earthly masters with fear and trembling, in singleness of heart, as you obey Christ; not only while being watched, and in order to please them, but as slaves of Christ, doing the will of God from the heart." (Ephesians 6:5–6)

"Tell slaves to be submissive to their masters and to give satisfaction in every respect; they are not to talk back, not to pilfer, but to show complete and perfect fidelity, so that in everything they may be an ornament to the doctrine of God our Savior." (Titus 2:9–10)

"Slaves, accept the authority of your masters with all deference, not only those who are kind and gentle but also those who are harsh. For it is a credit to you if, being aware of God, you endure pain while suffering unjustly. If you endure when you are beaten for doing wrong, what credit is that? But if you endure when you do right and suffer for it, you have God's approval." (1 Peter 2:18–20)

Appendices, Continued

Appendix IV

Constitutional Amendments

For the first ten amendments (the Bill of Rights), see Chapter 6, Bill of Rights.

AMENDMENT XI – Determines Rules for Suing States

Passed by Congress March 4, 1794.
Ratified February 7, 1795.

The Judicial power of the United States shall not be construed to extend to any suit in law or equity, commenced or prosecuted against one of the United States by Citizens of another State, or by Citizens or Subjects of any Foreign State.

AMENDMENT XII – Establishes Method for Presidential Election

Passed by Congress December 9, 1803.
Ratified June 15, 1804.

The Electors shall meet in their respective states and vote by ballot for President and Vice-President, one of whom, at least, shall not be an inhabitant of the same state with themselves; they shall name in their ballots the person voted for as President, and in distinct ballots the person voted for as Vice-President, and they shall make distinct lists of all persons voted for as President, and of all persons voted for as Vice-President, and of the number of votes for each, which lists they shall sign and certify, and transmit sealed to the seat of the government of the United States, directed to the President of the Senate; — the President of the Senate shall, in the presence of the Senate and House of Representatives, open all the certificates and the votes shall then be counted; — The person having the greatest number of votes for President, shall be the President, if such number be a majority of the whole number of Electors appointed; and if no person have such majority, then from the persons having the highest numbers not exceeding three on the list of those voted for as President, the House of Representatives shall choose immediately, by ballot, the President. But in choosing the President, the votes shall be taken by states, the representation from each state having one vote; a quorum for this purpose shall consist of a member or members from two-thirds of the states, and a majority of all the states shall be necessary to a choice. [And if the House of Representatives shall not choose a President whenever the right of choice shall devolve upon them, before the fourth day of March next following, then the Vice-President shall act as President, as in case of the death or other constitutional disability of the President. —]* The person having the greatest number of votes as Vice-President, shall be the Vice-President, if such number be a majority of the whole number of Electors appointed, and if no person have a majority, then from the two highest numbers on the list, the Senate shall choose the Vice-President; a quorum for the purpose shall consist of two-thirds of the whole number of Senators, and a majority of the whole number shall be necessary to a choice. But no person constitutionally ineligible to the office of President shall be eligible to that of Vice-President of the United States.

*Superseded by section 3 of the 20th amendment.

AMENDMENT XIII – Abolishes Slavery

Passed by Congress January 31, 1865. Ratified December 6, 1865.

Section 1.

Neither slavery nor involuntary servitude, except as a punishment for crime whereof the party shall have been duly convicted, shall exist within the United States, or any place subject to their jurisdiction.

AMENDMENT XIV – Grants Citizenship to Former Slaves

Passed by Congress June 13, 1866. Ratified July 9, 1868.

Section 1.

All persons born or naturalized in the United States, and subject to the jurisdiction thereof, are citizens of the United States and of the State wherein they reside. No State shall make or enforce any law which shall abridge the privileges or immunities of citizens of the United States; nor shall any State deprive any person of life, liberty, or property, without due process of law; nor deny to any person within its jurisdiction the equal protection of the laws.

AMENDMENT XV – Grants Black Males the Right to Vote

Passed by Congress February 26, 1869. Ratified February 3, 1870.

Section 1.

The right of citizens of the United States to vote shall not be denied or abridged by the United States or by any State on account of race, color, or previous condition of servitude—

AMENDMENT XVI – Establishes Income Taxes

Passed by Congress July 2, 1909. Ratified February 3, 1913.

The Congress shall have power to lay and collect taxes on incomes, from whatever source derived, without apportionment among the several States, and without regard to any census or enumeration.

AMENDMENT XVII – Establishes Direct Elections of Senators

Passed by Congress May 13, 1912. Ratified April 8, 1913.

The Senate of the United States shall be composed of two Senators from each State, elected by the people thereof, for six years; and each Senator shall have one vote. The electors in each State shall have the qualifications requisite for electors of the most numerous branch of the State legislatures.

Appendices, Continued

When vacancies happen in the representation of any State in the Senate, the executive authority of such State shall issue writs of election to fill such vacancies: *Provided*, That the legislature of any State may empower the executive thereof to make temporary appointments until the people fill the vacancies by election as the legislature may direct.

This amendment shall not be so construed as to affect the election or term of any Senator chosen before it becomes valid as part of the Constitution.

AMENDMENT XVIII – Makes Liquor Illegal

Passed by Congress December 18, 1917. Ratified January 16, 1919. Repealed by Amendment 21.

Section 1.
After one year from the ratification of this article the manufacture, sale, or transportation of intoxicating liquors within, the importation thereof into, or the exportation thereof from the United States and all territory subject to the jurisdiction thereof for beverage purposes is hereby prohibited.

Section 2.
The Congress and the several States shall have concurrent power to enforce this article by appropriate legislation.

Section 3.
This article shall be inoperative unless it shall have been ratified as an amendment to the Constitution by the legislatures of the several States, as provided in the Constitution, within seven years from the date

of the submission hereof to the States by the Congress.

AMENDMENT XIX – Grants Women the Right to Vote

Passed by Congress June 4, 1919. Ratified August 18, 1920.

The right of citizens of the United States to vote shall not be denied or abridged by the United States or by any State on account of sex.

AMENDMENT XX – Establishes Method of Assuming Office for President, Vice President, and Congress

Passed by Congress March 2, 1932. Ratified January 23, 1933.

Section 1.
The terms of the President and the Vice President shall end at noon on the 20th day of January, and the terms of Senators and Representatives at noon on the 3d day of January, of the years in which such terms would have ended if this article had not been ratified; and the terms of their successors shall then begin.

Section 2.
The Congress shall assemble at least once in every year, and such meeting shall begin at noon on the 3d day of January, unless they shall by law appoint a different day.

Section 3.
If, at the time fixed for the beginning of the term of the President, the President elect shall have died, the

Vice President elect shall become President. If a President shall not have been chosen before the time fixed for the beginning of his term, or if the President elect shall have failed to qualify, then the Vice President elect shall act as President until a President shall have qualified; and the Congress may by law provide for the case wherein neither a President elect nor a Vice President shall have qualified, declaring who shall then act as President, or the manner in which one who is to act shall be selected, and such person shall act accordingly until a President or Vice President shall have qualified.

Section 4.
The Congress may by law provide for the case of the death of any of the persons from whom the House of Representatives may choose a President whenever the right of choice shall have devolved upon them, and for the case of the death of any of the persons from whom the Senate may choose a Vice President whenever the right of choice shall have devolved upon them.

Section 5.
Sections 1 and 2 shall take effect on the 15th day of October following the ratification of this article.

Section 6.
This article shall be inoperative unless it shall have been ratified as an amendment to the Constitution by the legislatures of three-fourths of the several States within seven years from the date of its submission.

AMENDMENT XXI – Repeals Prohibition
Passed by Congress February 20, 1933. Ratified December 5, 1933.

Section 1.
The eighteenth article of amendment to the Constitution of the United States is hereby repealed.

Section 2.
The transportation or importation into any State, Territory, or Possession of the United States for delivery or use therein of intoxicating liquors, in violation of the laws thereof, is hereby prohibited.

Section 3.
This article shall be inoperative unless it shall have been ratified as an amendment to the Constitution by conventions in the several States, as provided in the Constitution, within seven years from the date of the submission hereof to the States by the Congress.

AMENDMENT XXII – Establishes Term Limits for the President
Passed by Congress March 21, 1947. Ratified February 27, 1951.

Section 1.
No person shall be elected to the office of the President more than twice, and no person who has held the office of President, or acted as President, for more than two years of a term to which some other person was elected President shall be elected to the office of President more than once. But this Article shall not apply to any person holding the office of

Appendices, Continued

President when this Article was proposed by Congress, and shall not prevent any person who may be holding the office of President, or acting as President, during the term within which this Article becomes operative from holding the office of President or acting as President during the remainder of such term.

Section 2.

This article shall be inoperative unless it shall have been ratified as an amendment to the Constitution by the legislatures of three-fourths of the several States within seven years from the date of its submission to the States by the Congress.

AMENDMENT XXIII – Establishes the Presidential Vote for Citizens of Washington D.C.

Passed by Congress June 16, 1960. Ratified March 29, 1961.

Section 1.

The District constituting the seat of Government of the United States shall appoint in such manner as Congress may direct:

A number of electors of President and Vice President equal to the whole number of Senators and Representatives in Congress to which the District would be entitled if it were a State, but in no event more than the least populous State; they shall be in addition to those appointed by the States, but they shall be considered, for the purposes of the election of President and Vice President, to be electors appointed by a State; and they shall meet in the District and perform such duties as provided by the twelfth article of amendment.

AMENDMENT XXIV – Bans Poll Taxes in Federal Elections

Passed by Congress August 27, 1962. Ratified January 23, 1964.

Section 1.

The right of citizens of the United States to vote in any primary or other election for President or Vice President, for electors for President or Vice President, or for Senator or Representative in Congress, shall not be denied or abridged by the United States or any State by reason of failure to pay poll tax or other tax.

AMENDMENT XXV – Establishes Rules for Presidential Disability

Passed by Congress July 6, 1965. Ratified February 10, 1967.

Section 1.

In case of the removal of the President from office or of his death or resignation, the Vice President shall become President.

Section 2.

Whenever there is a vacancy in the office of the Vice President, the President shall nominate a Vice President who shall take office upon confirmation by a majority vote of both Houses of Congress.

Section 3.

Whenever the President transmits to the President pro tempore of the Senate and the Speaker of the House of Representatives his written declaration that he is unable to discharge the powers and duties of

★ ★ ★ ★ ★ ★

his office, and until he transmits to them a written declaration to the contrary, such powers and duties shall be discharged by the Vice President as Acting President.

Section 4.

Whenever the Vice President and a majority of either the principal officers of the executive departments or of such other body as Congress may by law provide, transmit to the President pro tempore of the Senate and the Speaker of the House of Representatives their written declaration that the President is unable to discharge the powers and duties of his office, the Vice President shall immediately assume the powers and duties of the office as Acting President.

Thereafter, when the President transmits to the President pro tempore of the Senate and the Speaker of the House of Representatives his written declaration that no inability exists, he shall resume the powers and duties of his office unless the Vice President and a majority of either the principal officers of the executive department or of such other body as Congress may by law provide, transmit within four days to the President pro tempore of the Senate and the Speaker of the House of Representatives their written declaration that the President is unable to discharge the powers and duties of his office. Thereupon Congress shall decide the issue, assembling within forty-eight hours for that purpose if not in session. If the Congress, within twenty-one days after receipt of the latter written declaration, or, if Congress is not in session, within twenty-one days after Congress is required to assemble, determines by two-thirds vote of both Houses that the President is unable to discharge the powers and duties of his office, the Vice President shall continue to discharge the same as Acting President; otherwise, the President shall resume the powers and duties of his office.

AMENDMENT XXVI – Grants Voting Rights to Eighteen-Year-Olds

Passed by Congress March 23, 1971. Ratified July 1, 1971.

Section 1.

The right of citizens of the United States, who are eighteen years of age or older, to vote shall not be denied or abridged by the United States or by any State on account of age.

AMENDMENT XXVII – Establishes Limits on Congressional Pay Raises

Originally proposed September 25, 1789. Ratified May 7, 1992.

No law, varying the compensation for the services of the Senators and Representatives, shall take effect, until an election of representatives shall have intervened.

Appendices, Continued

Appendix V

Declaration of Independence

When in the Course of human events, it becomes necessary for one people to dissolve the political bands which have connected them with another, and to assume among the powers of the earth, the separate and equal station to which the Laws of Nature and of Nature's God entitle them, a decent respect to the opinions of mankind requires that they should declare the causes which impel them to the separation.

We hold these truths to be self-evident, that all men are created equal, that they are endowed by their Creator with certain unalienable Rights, that among these are Life, Liberty and the pursuit of Happiness.

That to secure these rights, Governments are instituted among Men, deriving their just powers from the consent of the governed,

That whenever any Form of Government becomes destructive of these ends, it is the Right of the People to alter or to abolish it, and to institute new Government, laying its foundation on such principles and organizing its powers in such form, as to them shall seem most likely to effect their Safety and Happiness. Prudence, indeed, will dictate that Governments long established should not be changed for light and transient causes; and accordingly all experience hath shown, that mankind are more disposed to suffer, while evils are sufferable than to right themselves by abolishing the forms to which they are accustomed. But when a long train of abuses and usurpations, pursuing invariably the same Object evinces a design to reduce them under absolute Despotism, it is their right, it is their duty, to throw off such Government, and to provide new Guards for their future security.

Such has been the patient sufferance of these Colonies; and such is now the necessity which constrains them to alter their former Systems of Government. The history of the present King of Great Britain is a history of repeated injuries and usurpations, all having in direct object the establishment of an absolute Tyranny over these States. To prove this, let Facts be submitted to a candid world.

He has refuted his Assent to Laws, the most wholesome and necessary for the public good.

He has forbidden his Governors to pass Laws of immediate and pressing importance, unless suspended in their operation till his Assent should be obtained; and when so suspended, he has utterly neglected to attend to them.

He has refused to pass other Laws for the accommodation of large districts of people, unless those people would relinquish the right of Representation in the Legislature, a right inestimable to them and formidable to tyrants only.

He has called together legislative bodies at places unusual, uncomfortable, and distant from the depository of their public Records, for the sole purpose of fatiguing them into compliance with his measures.

He has dissolved Representative Houses repeatedly, for opposing with manly firmness his invasions on the rights of the people.

He has refused for a long time, after such dissolutions, to cause others to be elected, whereby the Legislative Powers, incapable of Annihilation, have returned to the People at large for their exercise; the State remaining in the mean time exposed to all the dangers of invasion from without, and convulsions within.

He has endeavoured to prevent the population of these States; for that purpose obstructing the Laws for Naturalization of Foreigners; refusing to pass others to encourage their migrations hither, and raising the conditions of new Appropriations of Lands.

He has obstructed the Administration of Justice by refusing his Assent to Laws for establishing Judiciary Powers.

He has made Judges dependent on his Will alone, for the tenure of their offices, and the amount and payment of their salaries.

He has erected a multitude of New Offices, and sent hither swarms of Officers to harass our people, and eat out their substance.

He has kept among us, in times of peace, Standing Armies without the Consent of our legislatures.

He has affected to render the Military independent of and superior to the Civil Power.

Appendices, Continued

He has combined with others to subject us to a jurisdiction foreign to our constitution, and unacknowledged by our laws; giving his Assent to their Acts of pretended Legislation: —

For quartering large bodies of armed troops among us:

For protecting them, by a mock Trial from punishment for any Murders which they should commit on the Inhabitants of these States:

For cutting off our Trade with all parts of the world:

For imposing Taxes on us without our Consent:

For depriving us in many cases, of the benefit of Trial by Jury:

For transporting us beyond Seas to be tried for pretended offences:

For abolishing the free System of English Laws in a neighbouring Province, establishing therein an Arbitrary government, and enlarging its Boundaries so as to render it at once an example and fit instrument for introducing the same absolute rule into these Colonies:

For taking away our Charters, abolishing our most valuable Laws and altering fundamentally the Forms of our Governments:

For suspending our own Legislatures, and declaring themselves invested with power to legislate for us in all cases whatsoever.

He has abdicated Government here, by declaring us out of his Protection and waging War against us.

He has plundered our seas, ravaged our coasts, burnt our towns, and destroyed the lives of our people.

He is at this time transporting large Armies of foreign Mercenaries to compleat the works of death, desolation, and tyranny, already begun with circumstances of Cruelty & perfidy scarcely parallelled in the most barbarous ages, and totally unworthy the Head of a civilized nation.

He has constrained our fellow Citizens taken Captive on the high Seas to bear Arms against their Country, to become the executioners of their friends and Brethren, or to fall themselves by their Hands.

He has excited domestic insurrections amongst us, and has endeavoured to bring on the inhabitants of our frontiers, the merciless Indian Savages whose known rule of warfare, is an undistinguished destruction of all ages, sexes and conditions.

In every stage of these Oppressions We have Petitioned for Redress in the most humble terms: Our repeated Petitions have been answered only by repeated injury. A Prince, whose character is thus marked by every act which may define a Tyrant, is unfit to be the ruler of a free people.

Nor have We been wanting in attentions to our British brethren. We have warned them from time to time of attempts by their legislature to extend an unwarrantable jurisdiction over us. We have reminded them of the circumstances of our emigration and settlement here. We have appealed to their native justice and magnanimity, and we have conjured them by the ties of our common kindred to disavow these usurpations, which would inevitably interrupt our connections and correspondence. They too have been deaf to the voice of justice and of consanguinity. We must, therefore, acquiesce in the necessity, which denounces our Separation, and hold them, as we hold the rest of mankind, Enemies in War, in Peace Friends.

We, therefore, the Representatives of the United States of America, in General Congress, Assembled, appealing to the Supreme Judge of the world for the rectitude of our intentions, do, in the Name, and by Authority of the good People of these Colonies, solemnly publish and declare, That these United Colonies are, and of Right ought to be Free and Independent States; that they are Absolved from all Allegiance to the British Crown, and that all political connection between them and the State of Great Britain, is and ought to be totally dissolved; and that as Free and Independent States, they have full Power to levy War, conclude Peace contract Alliances, establish Commerce, and to do all other Acts and Things which Independent States may of right do. And for the support of this Declaration, with a firm reliance on the protection of divine Providence, we mutually pledge to each other our Lives, our Fortunes and our sacred Honor.

Appendices, Continued

Appendix VI

List of U.S. Presidents

1	Washington, George	(1789–97)	23	Harrison, Benjamin	(1889–93)
2	Adams, John	(1797–1801)	24	Cleveland, Grover	(1893–97)
3	Jefferson, Thomas	(1801–9)	25	McKinley, William	(1897–1901)
4	Madison, James	(1809–17)	26	Roosevelt, Theodore	(1901–9)
5	Monroe, James	(1817–25)	27	Taft, William Howard	(1909–13)
6	Adams, John Quincy	(1825–29)	28	Wilson, Woodrow	(1913–21)
7	Jackson, Andrew	(1829–37)	29	Harding, Warren Gamaliel	(1921–23)
8	Van Buren, Martin	(1837–41)	30	Coolidge, Calvin	(1923–29)
9	Harrison, William Henry	(1841)	31	Hoover, Herbert Clark	(1929–33)
10	Tyler, John	(1841–45)	32	Roosevelt, Franklin Delano	(1933–45)
11	Polk, James Knox	(1845–49)	33	Truman, Harry	(1945–53)
12	Taylor, Zachary	(1849–50)	34	Eisenhower, Dwight David	(1953–61)
13	Fillmore, Millard	(1850–53)	35	Kennedy, John Fitzgerald	(1961–63)
14	Pierce, Franklin	(1853–57)	36	Johnson, Lyndon Baines	(1963–69)
15	Buchanan, James	(1857–61)	37	Nixon, Richard Milhous	(1969–74)
16	Lincoln, Abraham	(1861–65)	38	Ford, Gerald Rudolph	(1974–77)
17	Johnson, Andrew	(1865–69)	39	Carter, James Earl Jr.	(1977–01)
18	Grant, Ulysses S.	(1869–77)	40	Reagan, Ronald Wilson	(1981–89)
19	Hayes, Rutherford Birchard	(1877–81)	41	Bush, George Herbert Walker	(1989–93)
20	Garfield, James Abram	(1881)	42	Clinton, William Jefferson	(1993–2001)
21	Arthur, Chester Alan	(1881–85)	43	Bush, George Walker	(2001–present)
22	Cleveland, Grover	(1885–89)			

Acknowledgments

First of all, Flocabulary would like to thank several people for their incredible artistic contributions to this project: Akir, Trajik, Lady BLADE, Grey, April Hill, Marty Keiser, Jon Froehlich, Slantize, Ed Boyer, Dr. Dr. Bob, and Da Cypha. A special shout-out to Jay Lifton who helped polish things up at the last minute. Thanks to Tim and Tony at Blink Music for their masterful touch.

We'd like to thank John Whalen, Buz Teacher, and Herb Rappaport for guiding us through the publishing process. We would also like to thank Tim Vaill for helping us fill the cupboards during production.

We'd like to thank our families—Tessa, Devon, Heather, Allison, Amanda, Matt, Margaret, Julia, Charlie, Lisbeth—for inspiring us to look deeper, but especially for their love and support.

Shout-out to Derek Etkin, who came up with the whole idea for track number 10, Big Ballin' (in the Gilded Age), back in Mrs. Zimmerman's class in 10th grade. Big thanks to Kenneth Davis, author of *Don't Know Much About History*, for writing that inspiring work.

Most of all, we'd like to thank all of the open-minded teachers out there who encouraged, criticized, and inspired us. Whenever we visit a school, we're continually amazed by teachers who go so far beyond what is required of them, just to reach students. This project is dedicated to your hard work, creativity, and dedication. Thank you.

121

Music Credits

1. Who Discovered It?
 Lyrics: Harrison
 Music: Rappaport (ASCAP)
 Vocals: Escher, Grey, Jon Froehlich,
 Marty Keiser

2. I Want America
 Lyrics: Harrison, Akir
 Music: Da Cypha
 Vocals: Akir, Escher, April Hill
 Sample: Margie Jospeh, *That Other
  Woman Got My Man and Gone,*
  Appears courtesy of Stax Records
  and Fantasy Jazz.

3. This Ain't Working
 Lyrics: Harrison
 Music: Rappaport
 Vocals: Escher, April Hill

**4. The Declaration of Independence
 (Interlude)**
 Lyrics: Thomas Jefferson
 Music: Rappaport
 Vocals: Escher

5. It's the U.S. (Bust the A)
 Lyrics: Harrison
 Music: Rappaport
 Vocals: Escher, Marty Keiser

6. Bill of Rights
 Lyrics: Harrison
 Music: Rappaport/Keiser
 Vocals: Escher

7. O.D.W.M.
 Lyrics: Harrison
 Music: Shadowville Productions/Slantize
 Vocals: Escher, Trajik

8. Frederick and Abraham (Interlude)
 Lyrics: Frederick Douglass, Abraham
  Lincoln
 Music: Rappaport
 Vocals: Escher, Jon Froehlich

9. Ghosts of the Civil War
 Lyrics: Grey, Lady BLADE, Harrison
 Music: Rappaport
 Vocals: Grey, Escher, Lady BLADE
 This song was partially inspiered by
 Eminem's "My Name Is".

★ ★ ★ ★ ★ ★

10. *Big Ballin' (in the Gilded Age)*
   Lyrics: Harrison, Grey, Trajik
   Music: Ed Boyer
   Vocals: Escher, Trajik, Grey

11. *Jazz Age*
   Lyrics: Harrison
   Music: Dr. Dr. Bob
   Vocals: Escher

12. *FDR (Interlude)*
   Lyrics: Franklin Delano Roosevelt
   Music: Rappaport
   Vocals: Escher

13. *Would You Drop It?*
   Lyrics: Harrison
   Music: Rappaport
   Vocals: Escher

14. *Let Freedom Ring*
   Lyrics: Martin Luther King Jr.,
      Harrison, Trajik
   Music: Rappaport
   Vocals: MLK, Trajik, Escher
   Sample: Excerpts from "I have a
      dream" appear courtesy of the
      King Estate.

All music recorded at Flocabulary
Studios, New York, NY
Music production by Alex Rappaport
and Blake Harrison
Engineered by Alex Rappaport
Mastered by Tim Lukas at Blink Music
Published by Escher Robinson Music
(ASCAP)

Bibliography

Ambrose, Stephen. *Undaunted Courage: Meriwether Lewis, Thomas Jefferson, and the Opening of the American West.* New York: Simon & Schuster, 1996.

Chernow, Ron. *The House of Morgan: An American Banking Dynasty and the Rise of Modern American Finance.* New York: Grove Press, 1990.

Ibid. *Titan: The Life of John D. Rockefeller.* New York: Random House, 1998.

Colbert, David, ed. *Eyewitness to America: 500 Years of American History in the Words of Those Who Saw It Happen.* New York: Pantheon, 1997.

Davis, Kenneth C. *Don't Know Much About History.* New York: HarperCollins, 2003.

Diamond, Jared. *Guns, Germs and Steel: The Fates of Human Societies.* New York: Norton, 1998.

Douglass, Frederick. *Narrative of the Life of Frederick Douglass.* New York: Signet, 1968.

Fleming, Thomas. *Duel: Alexander Hamilton, Aaron Burr, and the Future of America.* New York: Basic Books, 1999.

Ibid. *Liberty! The American Revolution.* New York: Viking, 1997.

Franklin, Benjamin. *The Autobiography and Other Writings.* New York: Signet, 1961.

Garrow, David J. *Bearing the Cross: Martin Luther King, Jr., and the Southern Christian Leadership Conference.* New York: Morrow, 1986.

Hakim, Joy. *From Colonies to Country.* New York: Oxford University Press, 1985.

Hersey, John. *Hiroshima.* New York: Knopf, 1946.

Hoxie, Frederick E., ed. *Encyclopedia of North American Indians*. Boston: Houghton Mifflin, 1996.

McCullough, David. *1776*. New York: Simon & Schuster, 2005.

McPherson, James M. *Battle Cry of Freedom: The Civil War Era*. London: Oxford University Press, 1988.

Paine, Thomas. *Common Sense, The Rights of Man and Other Essential Writings*. New York: Meridian, 1984.

Sparknotes SAT U.S. History. New York: Spark Publishing, 2005.

United States History: Preparing for the Advanced Placement Examination. New York: Amsco School Publications, 1998.

X, Malcolm, with Alex Haley. *The Autobiography of Malcolm X*. New York: Grove Press, 1964.

Zinn, Howard. *A People's History of the United States*. New York: Harper & Row, 1980.

Photo and Illustration Credits

Chapter 1, page 8, 14, 15—*The landing of Columbus* 1492, by Buek, 1893

Chapter 2, page 16, 22, 23—*The wedding of Pocahontas with John Rolfe.* Lithograph by Jospeh Hoover, 1867.

Chapter 3, page 24. 28, 29—*The "Minute-Men" of the Revolution.* Lithograph by Currier & Ives, 1876.

page 27—*The destruction of tea at Boston harbor.* Lithograph by N. Currier, 1846.

Chapter 4, page 32, 34—*John Hancock's defiance*, July 4, 1776. Lithograph by Currier & Ives, 1876.

Chapter 5, page 36, 41—*Washington and his generals.* Engraving by Alexander H. Ritchie.

Chapter 6, page 42, 45, 46—First Amendment: Right to Protest [*Protest Against Child Labor in a Labor Parade,* 1909], Bain News Service photograph.

Chapter 7, page 48, 50—*Thomas Jefferson, third president of the United States.* Pendleton's Lithography. Created/Published 1828.

Chapter 8, page 56—Frederick Douglass, Photograph.

page 58—*Photograph of President Lincoln and Thomas (Tad)* by Mathew B. Brady, 1864.

Chapter 9, page 60—*The discovery of Nat Turner* by E. Benjamin Andrews, 1895.

page 62—*J.C. Calhoun,* 1823. Mathew B. Brady, photographer.

page 64—*Harriet Tubman. (Full length).* Photograph by H. B. Lindsley

page 68—*The assassination of President Lincoln at Ford's Theatre, Washington, D.C.,* April 14th, 1865. Currier & Ives.

Chapter 10, page 70—*I gave credit. I sell for cash.* Lithograph by Currier & Ives, 1870.

Chapter 11, page 78—*Portrait of Langston Hughes,* 1943. GordonParks, photographer.

Chapter 12, page 82—*Migrant agricultural worker's family,* 1936. Dorothea Lange, photographer.

Chapter 13, page 84—*Roosevelt, Stalin, and Churchill on portico of Russian Embassy in Teheran, during conference, Nov. 28 - Dec. 1, 1943.* U.S. Signal Corps photo

page 86—*Adolf Hitler In Nuremberg.* Halftone photomechanical print from cigarette card. 1923.

Chapter 14, page 92—*Martin Luther King, Jr., at a press conference at the Capitol, Washington, D.C.* Photograph by Marion S. Trikosko, 1964.

About the Authors

Blake Harrison and Alex Rappaport founded Flocabulary in 2004. Other works by the authors include *Flocabulary: The Hip-Hop Approach to SAT-Level Vocabulary Building (2005)* and *The Rapper's Handbook (2006)*. Flocabulary has appeared in international press and its music can be found in classrooms across the world. Both Blake and Alex live in New York City.

About Cider Mill Press Book Publishers

Good ideas ripen with time. From seed to harvest, Cider Mill Press strives to bring fine reading, information, and entertainment together between the covers of its creatively crafted books. Our Cider Mill bears fruit twice a year, publishing a new crop of titles each spring and fall.

Visit us on the web at
www.cidermillpress.com
or write to us at
12 Port Farm Road
Kennebunkport, Maine 04046

CIDER MILL
PRESS

BOOK
PUBLISHERS

*Where Good Books
are Ready for Press*

Notes

Notes